Journey into Data Science and Machine Learning

Data-Driven Decision Making: Harnessing the Power of Machine Learning

Gabriel Chen

Table of Contents

INTRODUCTION

As the digital world continues to change, data is becoming the new currency of the modern world. Large volumes of data are being gathered by organizations of all sizes, encompassing everything from operational statistics and market trends to customer preferences and behavior. But the real value of this data comes from turning it into insights that can be put into practice, not just from the amount of data gathered. Here's where machine learning and data science come into play.

Welcome to "Journey into Data Science and Machine Learning: Data-Driven Decision Making - Harnessing the Power of Machine Learning." We go on a tour through the dynamic domains of data-driven decision-making and machine learning's transformative potential in this extensive e-book. Our goal is to provide you with the skills and information required to effectively negotiate this fascinating environment and take use of its potential to help you make wise decisions.

The subsequent pages aim to simplify the intricate ideas surrounding data science and machine learning, giving you a strong basis to confidently go into these domains. We will explore the complex procedures that transform unprocessed data into meaningful insights, explore the inner workings of different machine learning algorithms, and comprehend how these technologies are transforming global companies.

We establish the basis in the first few chapters by exploring the fundamentals of machine learning and data science. We'll go through their history, define important terms, and see how important data-driven decision-making is in the current competitive landscape.

We'll walk you through every step of the data science process as we go along, from problem definition and data collection to exploratory analysis and the identification of significant patterns. We'll explore the intricacies of feature engineering, an essential stage that can greatly influence machine learning models' efficacy.

After gaining a firm grasp of the fundamentals, we will navigate the world of machine learning algorithms. We will address both supervised and unsupervised learning strategies, and you will get knowledge on how to choose, develop, and assess models successfully. We'll also look at deep learning and neural networks, which are advancing fields like image identification and natural language processing, among others.

However, the adventure doesn't end with model training. The practical aspects of implementing machine learning models in real-world applications are covered in this e-book. You'll learn what factors to take into account for a successful deployment, as well as for ongoing maintenance and monitoring to make sure your models keep producing value over time.

However, enormous power also entails considerable responsibility. The significance of ethical problems and biases in data science cannot be overstated. We'll dig into the difficulties posed by algorithmic bias and the moral implications of data gathering and usage, making sure you're equipped to handle these important issues.
As we move forward, case studies from the actual world will help us visualize the ideas. These examples will demonstrate how deep learning techniques and data

science have been used to address real-world problems in a variety of industries, from manufacturing's predictive maintenance to medical diagnosis.

Lastly, we'll look ahead and investigate new developments as well as the use of AI across a range of industries. Since this field is always evolving, we'll close with a call to continued learning and skill growth.

Get ready to gain the skills and understanding needed to fully utilize data science and machine learning. This e-book is your entry point to the world of data-driven decision-making, regardless of whether you're a business professional looking for data-driven methods, a student hoping to enter the industry, or anybody else fascinated by the possibilities of technology.

Together, let's take this insightful journey to realize the enormous potential that exists at the center of innovation, technology, and data.

CHAPTER I

Foundations of Data Science and Machine Learning

Understanding Data Science and Machine Learning

In the modern age of information, the volume of data generated on a daily basis is staggering. This deluge of data has given rise to disciplines like Data Science and Machine Learning, which hold the key to transforming raw information into actionable insights, enabling informed decision-making across various domains. Data Science and Machine Learning are interconnected world that synergize the power of data with sophisticated algorithms, driving innovation and efficiency in industries worldwide.

Data Science, at its core, is the art of extracting knowledge and insights from complex and unstructured data. It encompasses a multidisciplinary approach that amalgamates expertise from statistics, computer science, domain knowledge, and data visualization. The primary goal of data science is to uncover patterns, trends, and correlations within data, offering organizations a deeper understanding of their operations, customers, and markets. The data science process involves several key steps: defining the problem, collecting and preprocessing data, performing exploratory data analysis, and building predictive models. This process empowers businesses to derive actionable insights from data, enabling them to optimize processes, enhance customer experiences, and innovate in ways that were previously unattainable.

Machine Learning, conversely, is an artificial intelligence subset that lets computers to gain knowledge from data without being explicitly programmed. It's the driving force behind the automation of decision-making processes and the creation of predictive models. Machine learning algorithms is classified into three types: supervised, unsupervised, and reinforcement learning. Supervised learning involves training models on labeled data to make predictions or classifications, while unsupervised learning focuses on identifying patterns in unlabeled data. Reinforcement learning involves training models to make sequences of decisions depending on feedback from the environment. Machine learning is employed in various applications, from recommendation systems and fraud detection to autonomous vehicles and medical diagnoses.

It is indisputable that machine learning and data science work well together. The basis is provided by data science, which prepares and transforms data into a format that is appropriate for machine learning models. Feature engineering, a crucial aspect of data science, involves selecting, extracting, and transforming the most relevant features from the data to enhance the performance of machine learning algorithms. In turn, machine learning algorithms process this prepared data to learn patterns and relationships, making predictions and decisions that are far more accurate and scalable than traditional rule-based approaches.

One of the remarkable aspects of these fields is their ubiquitous presence. They extend their reach across industries such as finance, healthcare, marketing, and manufacturing. For instance, in healthcare, data science and machine learning are driving the development of personalized medicine, where treatment plans are tailored to an individual's genetic makeup and medical history. Similarly, e-commerce platforms leverage these technologies to provide personalized recommendations to users, enhancing user engagement and sales.

However, these fields are not without challenges. Data privacy and security concerns have intensified as the need for data collection and sharing grows. Ensuring that data is used ethically and without bias is a critical consideration. Bias in data or algorithms can lead to unfair or discriminatory outcomes, making it imperative for practitioners to actively mitigate these issues.

In conclusion, Data Science and Machine Learning have revolutionized the way we interact with data and make decisions. They empower organizations to harness the vast amounts of data available to them, transforming it into valuable insights that drive innovation and competitive advantage. As these fields continue to evolve, individuals and businesses must not only embrace their potential but also navigate the ethical and practical challenges that come with them. By doing so, we can truly unlock the transformative power of data and technology for the betterment of society as a whole.

Historical Overview of Data Science and Machine Learning

The roots of data science and machine learning extend deep into the annals of history, shaped by a confluence of mathematical theories, technological advancements, and the relentless pursuit of knowledge. These fields, which have now become integral to our modern world, have a rich historical tapestry that showcases the evolution of human understanding and the remarkable progression of computational capabilities.

The origins of data science can be traced back to the mid-20th century, when the burgeoning field of statistics began to intertwine with computer science. Pioneers like John Tukey and Peter Naur recognized the potential of data analysis with computers, paving the way for what we now call data science. Mainframe computers appearance in the 1960s facilitated the processing of larger datasets, spurring interest in data analysis techniques. The emergence of databases and data warehousing in the 1970s further fueled the growth of data management practices.

The concept of data mining gained traction in the 1980s and 1990s, as researchers sought ways to extract valuable information from large datasets. This era witnessed the development of algorithms for discovering patterns and trends within data, setting the stage for modern data science practices. With the rise of the internet, the 2000s saw an explosion of digital data, prompting the requirement for more sophisticated tools to manage and analyze this information. This marked the transition from data mining to the broader discipline of data science, encompassing data cleaning, preprocessing, analysis, and visualization.

Machine learning's history is intertwined with the very essence of artificial intelligence (AI). The seeds were sown in the 1950s and 1960s, when computer scientists and mathematicians envisioned creating machines that could mimic human intelligence. The concept of the "perceptron," a single-layer neural network, emerged during this time, although its limitations led to a period of reduced interest in neural networks.

In the 1980s and 1990s, machine learning experienced a renaissance as researchers developed more complex algorithms and techniques. Decision trees, support vector machines (or SVM), as well as clustering algorithms began to take shape. However, the lack of sufficient data and computational power limited the practical application of these methods.

The turn of the 21st century marked a significant turning point. The availability of massive datasets and the exponential growth of computing capabilities paved the way for the resurgence of neural networks and the birth of deep learning. In 2012, the ImageNet competition witnessed the triumph of deep convolutional neural networks, revolutionizing computer vision and sparking the deep learning revolution.

As the 21st century progressed, the boundaries between data science and machine learning blurred, with both fields benefiting from technological advancements. The growth of cloud computing and distributed computing frameworks facilitated the processing of vast amounts of data, while open-source libraries and tools democratized access to advanced algorithms.

Today, data science and machine learning are integral to diverse domains. In healthcare, predictive modeling aids in disease diagnosis, while in finance, algorithms drive high-frequency trading and risk assessment. Social media platforms leverage these technologies to personalize user experiences, and autonomous vehicles rely on machine learning for navigation and decision-making.

Yet, challenges persist. The ethical use of data, the potential for bias in algorithms, and the need for transparent decision-making remain focal points. As we look ahead, the fusion of data science and machine learning with other technologies like artificial intelligence, natural language processing, and robotics promises to shape a future where intelligent systems seamlessly integrate into our lives.

In conclusion, the historical journey of data science and machine learning reflects the persistent human quest to decipher patterns, unlock insights, and augment our understanding of the world. From the early days of statistics and AI to the modern era of big data and deep learning, these fields have transformed from theoretical concepts to practical tools that empower us to make informed decisions and propel innovation forward. As we continue to build upon this legacy, the narrative of data science and machine learning unfolds as a testament to the inexorable progress of human knowledge and the boundless possibilities that lie ahead.

Key Concepts and Terminology

In the complex realm of data science and machine learning, a tapestry of key concepts and terminology weaves together to create a comprehensive understanding of these disciplines. As the backbone of modern data-driven decision-making, these concepts form the foundation upon which data scientists and machine learning practitioners build their expertise. Let us delve into this world, unraveling the intricacies and uncovering the essential elements that drive the processes and methodologies within data science and machine learning.

At the heart of data science and machine learning lies data itself, the raw material from which insights are extracted. Data can be broadly classified into structured and unstructured forms. Structured data, organized into tables or databases, lends itself well to traditional analysis. On the other hand, unstructured data, comprising text, images, audio, and video, requires advanced techniques to derive meaningful insights.

Data has dimensions, known as features or variables. A feature is a measurable property of the phenomenon being observed. For example, in a customer dataset, features could include age, gender, purchase history, and geographic location. The number of features affects the complexity of analyses and models, emphasizing the importance of feature selection and engineering in optimizing performance.

Exploratory Data Analysis (EDA) is the process of visually and statistically summarizing data to uncover patterns, trends, and relationships. It involves techniques such as histograms, scatter plots, and correlation matrices to gain an initial understanding of the data's distribution and interdependencies. EDA is a crucial precursor to model building, as it guides feature selection and informs data preprocessing steps.

Feature Engineering is an art within data science that involves transforming raw data into meaningful features that improve the performance of machine learning models. It encompasses techniques like normalization, scaling, and one-hot encoding to ensure that data is in a suitable format for analysis. Feature engineering also involves creating new features based on domain knowledge, which can significantly impact model accuracy.

A machine learning paradigm where models learn from labeled data to make predictions or classifications, is known as supervised learning. Labeled data consists of input-output pairs, enabling the model to learn the connection between inputs and corresponding outputs. Common supervised learning algorithms include linear regression for regression tasks and logistic regression for binary classification tasks.

Unsupervised learning involves learning patterns from unlabeled data, making it particularly useful for data exploration and clustering. Clustering algorithms group similar data points together based on inherent patterns. An example of unsupervised learning is K-Means clustering, which partitions data into distinct clusters.

Once a model is trained, evaluating its performance is paramount. Common evaluation metrics vary based on the problem type. In classification, metrics like accuracy, precision, recall, and F1-score quantify the model's performance on predicting classes. In regression, metrics such as Mean Absolute Error (MAE) and Root Mean Squared Error (RMSE) assess the model's accuracy in predicting continuous values.

Overfitting refer to the case when a model learns the training data too well, capturing noise and outliers rather than general patterns. Regularization techniques, such as L1 (Lasso) and L2 (Ridge) regularization, mitigate overfitting by adding penalty terms to the model's parameters. These penalties discourage extreme parameter values, resulting in a more generalized model.

Bias in data and algorithms is a critical concern in data science and machine learning. It occurs when data collection or model training processes inadvertently favor certain groups, leading to unfair outcomes. Ensuring fairness requires careful data collection, preprocessing, and algorithm design to minimize biases and promote equitable decision-making.

Deploying a machine learning model involves transitioning it from a development environment to a production environment where it can make real-time predictions. Scalability considerations, such as handling high traffic and maintaining model performance, play a pivotal role in successful deployment. Techniques like containerization and cloud services facilitate efficient deployment.

Data science and machine learning also intersect with ethical considerations. The vast amounts of data collected raise concerns about privacy and informed consent. Responsible data usage involves anonymizing data, obtaining user consent, and adhering to regulations like GDPR.

In conclusion, the landscape of data science and machine learning is adorned with a rich tapestry of concepts and terminology. From data exploration and feature engineering to model evaluation and ethical considerations, each thread contributes to the intricate fabric of knowledge that guides practitioners in harnessing the power of data. Understanding these key concepts equips us to navigate the challenges and opportunities presented by data-driven decision-making and machine learning, ensuring that we wield these transformative tools responsibly and effectively.

CHAPTER II

The Data Science Process

Steps of the Data Science Process

In the digital age, data has become the driving force behind innovation and decision-making across industries. The process of extracting meaningful insights from data, known as the data science process, is a systematic journey that blends technical expertise, domain knowledge, and analytical skills. This process encompasses a series of well-defined steps that guide practitioners from problem formulation to actionable insights, enabling them to navigate the vast sea of data with purpose and precision. Let us embark on this journey through the steps of the data science process, unraveling the intricacies and highlighting the significance of each phase.

Step 1: Problem Definition and Understanding:

The data science process begins with a clear articulation of the problem at hand. Understanding the problem's context, objectives, and potential impact is essential. This involves collaborating closely with domain experts and stakeholders to ensure that the analysis aligns with organizational goals. The clarity achieved at this stage sets the foundation for the subsequent steps.

Step 2: Data Collection:

With the problem defined, the next step involves gathering relevant data. Data can come from a variety of sources, including databases, APIs, and external datasets. Ensuring the data's quality and integrity is paramount, as the accuracy of insights hinges on the quality of input data. This phase may require data cleaning to address missing values, outliers, and inconsistencies that could distort analyses.

Step 3: Data Preprocessing:

Raw data often requires preprocessing before analysis. This step involves transforming, cleaning, and structuring the data for analysis. Techniques like data normalization, feature scaling, and one-hot encoding are employed to ensure data consistency and comparability. This phase lays the groundwork for subsequent analysis by ensuring that the data is in a suitable format.

Step 4: Exploratory Data Analysis (EDA):

Exploratory Data Analysis is a crucial step that involves delving into the data's patterns, distributions, and relationships. This process employs visualizations, statistical summaries, and correlation analyses to uncover insights that inform subsequent decisions. EDA aids in feature selection, identification of outliers, and a deeper understanding of the data's nuances.

Step 5: Feature Engineering:

This is the process of selecting, transforming, and creating relevant features that enhance the predictive power of machine learning models. Domain knowledge plays a vital role here, as practitioners leverage their understanding of the problem to engineer features that capture meaningful patterns. This step requires creativity and a deep understanding of both the data and the problem domain.

Step 6: Model Selection and Training:

In this phase, suitable machine learning algorithms are chosen based on the nature of the problem, the data, and the desired outcomes. Supervised, unsupervised, or reinforcement learning algorithms may be selected. The chosen model is trained using labeled data, and parameters are tuned to achieve optimal performance. This step requires iterative refinement to find the best-fitting model.

Step 7: Model Evaluation:

Once a model is trained, it needs to be evaluated to assess its performance. This involves using validation datasets and metrics to quantify the model's accuracy, precision, recall, and other relevant measures. Model evaluation helps identify potential overfitting, where a model performs properly on training data but poorly on new, unseen data.

Step 8: Model Deployment and Monitoring:

A successful model must transition from the development to a production environment, where it can make real-time predictions. This involves deploying the model on servers or cloud platforms and integrating it into existing systems. Additionally, ongoing monitoring is crucial to ensure that the model continues to perform accurately and efficiently in real-world scenarios.

Step 9: Interpretation and Communication of Results:

The insights derived from the model need to be interpreted and communicated effectively to stakeholders. This step involves translating complex technical results into actionable insights that can drive informed decision-making. Clear and concise visualization techniques, along with domain-specific context, help convey the significance of the findings.

Step 10: Iteration and Continuous Improvement: The data

science process is not a linear path but rather a cycle of continuous improvement. After deploying the model and gaining insights, feedback and new data may lead to the refinement of the problem definition, preprocessing steps, or even the choice of algorithms. This iterative approach ensures that solutions remain relevant and effective as conditions evolve.

In conclusion, the data science process is a structured journey that transforms raw data into valuable insights. Each step, from problem definition and data collection to model deployment and continuous improvement, plays a vital role in extracting knowledge from data. By navigating through these steps with meticulous attention to detail and an in-depth understanding of the problem domain, data scientists pave the way for informed decision-making, innovation, and progress across a spectrum of industries.

Defining the Problem and Setting Objectives

The journey of data science is an intricate one, driven by the pursuit of insights from vast and complex datasets.

At the heart of this journey lies the critical initial step: defining the problem and setting clear objectives. This foundational phase lays the groundwork for the entire data science process, guiding practitioners through the intricacies of data collection, analysis, and interpretation. In this section, we delve into the significance of problem definition and objective setting, exploring how these aspects shape the trajectory of data-driven endeavors and pave the way for impactful outcomes.

The process commences with a pivotal question: What problem needs solving? Problem definition is not merely about identifying an issue; it's about crafting a well-defined question that frames the scope and purpose of the analysis. It requires collaboration between data scientists and domain experts to gain a profound understanding of the problem's context, nuances, and potential impact. Without a well-defined problem, data analysis risks being aimless, leading to insights that may not align with organizational goals.

Clear problem definition serves as a guiding light, steering the subsequent steps of the data science process. It narrows the focus, ensuring that efforts are channeled towards pertinent aspects. For instance, in a business scenario, problem definition might involve pinpointing the factors influencing customer churn. In healthcare, it could revolve around predicting disease outcomes based on patient data. Defining the problem also aids in selecting appropriate data sources and techniques, thus maximizing the efficiency of the data science endeavor.

Setting clear objectives follows naturally from problem definition. Objectives specify the goals of the analysis— what insights are sought, and how they align with the problem at hand. These objectives provide a quantifiable framework against which the success of the analysis can be measured. Objectives can range from predicting future trends and identifying patterns to classifying data points or optimizing processes.

Objectives lend direction to the entire data science process. They influence the choice of algorithms, the design of experiments, and the selection of evaluation metrics. For example, if the objective is to minimize false positives in a medical diagnosis model, the focus shifts towards optimizing precision. Conversely, if the goal is to detect rare events, recall might take precedence. Objectives guide decisions and methodologies, ensuring that the analysis remains purposeful and outcomes-oriented.

The intricate interplay between problem definition and objective setting underscores their significance. Together, they prevent the "solution looking for a problem" pitfall, where analysis begins without a clear sense of purpose. They channel efforts towards extracting insights that are not only technically accurate but also aligned with the broader organizational goals. A well-defined problem and clear objectives serve as a litmus test for the relevance and applicability of the analysis.

Moreover, these aspects foster effective communication and collaboration. Domain experts, who possess contextual knowledge, play a pivotal role in refining problem statements and shaping objectives. This collaboration bridges the gap between data science and real-world impact, ensuring that the insights gleaned have actionable implications. Well-defined problems and objectives transcend technical jargon, enabling data scientists to articulate their findings in terms that resonate with stakeholders.

Defining the problem and setting objectives is not without its challenges. Ambiguous problem statements can lead to misaligned analysis, while overly specific ones may miss broader insights. Balancing granularity and scope is a delicate task, requiring an in-depth understanding of both the domain and the available data. Furthermore, objectives should be realistic and achievable, accounting for the limitations of the data and resources.

Iterative refinement is often necessary as insights unfold. Feedback from stakeholders and evolving data might necessitate adjustments to problem definitions and objectives. Flexibility, coupled with a commitment to aligning the analysis with the problem's essence, ensures that the data science process remains agile and adaptive. In the symphony of data science, the first notes are composed through problem definition and objective setting. These initial steps set the tone, guiding the entire data analysis process towards meaningful outcomes.

They transform abstract challenges into structured questions, channeling efforts towards insights that transcend numbers and charts. Problem definition and objective setting underscore the essence of data science—bridging the gap between data and decision-making, between complexity and clarity. With these foundational pillars in place, the data science journey takes flight, charting a course towards insights that drive innovation, efficiency, and progress.

Data Collection and Preprocessing

In the vast landscape of data science, where information flows ceaselessly from a multitude of sources, the processes of data collection and preprocessing emerge as the bedrock upon which insights are constructed. The transfer from raw data to actionable insights is intricate and demanding, requiring meticulous attention to detail and an in-depth understanding of the complexities of the data. This section delves into the fundamental phases of data collection and preprocessing, unraveling their significance, challenges, and transformative role in shaping the data science narrative.

Data collection is the gateway to the world of data science. It involves gathering relevant data from diverse sources, be it databases, APIs, web scraping, or sensor networks. The data collected can span structured or unstructured forms, ranging from numerical records to text, images, audio, and video. The choice of data sources is influenced by the problem's context, the available resources, and the data's quality.

The significance of data collection cannot be overstated. The quality, completeness, and relevance of the data serve as the foundation upon which subsequent analyses are built. The adage "garbage in, garbage out" aptly illustrates the critical importance of starting with accurate and reliable data. A rigorous approach to data collection ensures that the insights derived are credible and actionable, preventing inaccuracies and misleading conclusions.

Raw data is rarely pristine—it often comes with imperfections, inconsistencies, and noise. Data preprocessing is the process of refining and structuring the raw data to make it suitable for analysis. This phase involves a series of tasks, including data cleaning, data transformation, feature extraction, and feature scaling. Data cleaning addresses issues like missing values, duplicates, and outliers that can skew analysis results. Imputing missing values, for instance, requires making informed decisions about the best way to estimate or replace them. Duplicates and outliers can distort statistical summaries and lead to inaccurate insights.

Data transformation involves reshaping the data to better suit the analysis. This might involve aggregating data, encoding categorical variables, and normalizing features. Feature extraction is the process of creating novel features from existing data, often leveraging domain knowledge to capture relevant patterns. Feature scaling ensures that numerical features are on similar scales, preventing certain features from disproportionately influencing the analysis due to their magnitude.

Data collection and preprocessing are laden with challenges. Data collection can be constrained by factors such as data availability, accessibility, and privacy concerns. Obtaining high-quality data can be resource-intensive, requiring collaboration with domain experts and stakeholders to ensure the data's relevance.
Data preprocessing, though critical, is not without its complexities. Deciding how to handle missing data, outliers, and categorical variables involves making subjective choices that can impact the analysis's outcomes. Data transformation introduces the potential for information loss or distortion, necessitating a delicate balance between preserving relevant information and enhancing analysis capabilities.

Moreover, scalability is a consideration when dealing with large datasets. Ensuring that preprocessing steps are efficient and do not consume excessive computational resources is crucial, especially in big data contexts.
Data preprocessing is akin to refining raw materials before crafting a masterpiece. Its transformative power

cannot be overstated. Raw data, often fragmented and disorderly, is honed into a structured form that can reveal hidden patterns, trends, and insights. Without preprocessing, analyses might be riddled with noise and distortions, leading to erroneous conclusions.

Feature extraction, a facet of preprocessing, is particularly noteworthy. By engineering features that encapsulate domain-specific knowledge, practitioners imbue the data with context, enhancing the analysis's accuracy and interpretability. This step transforms raw data into a conduit through which real-world understanding is channeled.

Data collection and preprocessing are the foundational pillars of the data science journey. They demand meticulousness, domain expertise, and a commitment to data integrity. The quality of the data collected and the rigor of the preprocessing phase are decisive factors that shape the accuracy and reliability of insights. As data sources proliferate and data complexity grows, the art of data collection and the science of data preprocessing remain paramount. In this intricate dance of data, where raw materials are refined and transformed into insights, the data scientist's role as an alchemist comes to life, turning data into gold through the alchemy of knowledge and skill.

Exploratory Data Analysis (EDA)

In the realm of data science, where vast troves of information lie waiting to be unraveled, the process of Exploratory Data Analysis (EDA) emerges as a powerful beacon. EDA is not just a precursor to analysis; it is a dynamic journey of discovery, a compass that guides practitioners through the labyrinthine landscape of data.

In this section, we delve into the essence of Exploratory Data Analysis, uncovering its significance, methodologies, and transformative role in extracting insights from raw data.

Exploratory Data Analysis is the art of visually and statistically summarizing data to uncover patterns, relationships, anomalies, and potential insights. Unlike traditional analyses that begin with predefined hypotheses, EDA embraces curiosity-driven exploration. It allows data scientists to immerse themselves in the data, asking questions and seeking patterns that might not have been apparent initially.

The importance of EDA cannot be overstated. It provides an essential foundation for subsequent analyses, guiding decisions about model selection, feature engineering, and data preprocessing. EDA also acts as a safeguard against erroneous conclusions, as it enables the identification of outliers, errors, and inconsistencies that could distort the analysis.

EDA employs an array of techniques to illuminate the inherent structure of data. Visualizations, such as histograms, scatter plots, box plots, and heatmaps, transform numbers into visual patterns. These visualizations unveil distributions, correlations, and potential clusters within the data. Summary statistics like mean, median, and standard deviation provide snapshots of central tendencies and variability, offering a quantitative perspective.

Correlation analysis explores the relationships between variables, uncovering dependencies that inform subsequent analyses. Dimensionality reduction techniques such as PCA condense multidimensional data into lower dimensions while preserving relevant information. These techniques enrich the data scientist's toolkit, enabling nuanced interpretations and deeper insights.

EDA is not a linear process; it's an evolving journey of discovery. It commences with a general overview, acquainting data scientists with the data's characteristics. This is followed by the identification of patterns, relationships, and potential outliers. As insights emerge, the focus narrows, delving deeper into specific aspects. Iterative cycles of EDA refine the understanding of the data, driving the formulation of hypotheses and informing subsequent analyses. Patterns that surface in early iterations might lead to questions that prompt further exploration. This iterative nature ensures that the insights gleaned are comprehensive and holistic, capturing the data's multifaceted essence.

EDA transforms raw data into actionable insights, much like a sculptor shapes a block of stone into a masterpiece. By visualizing data distributions and relationships, EDA elucidates trends that can guide business decisions, policy formulation, and scientific inquiries. It provides a visual narrative that resonates with stakeholders, fostering better communication of findings.

EDA also humanizes data, infusing it with context and relevance. Anomalies detected through EDA might lead to the discovery of data collection errors or significant events that necessitate further investigation. Moreover, EDA fosters creativity, allowing data scientists to question assumptions and challenge existing knowledge.

EDA is not without challenges. In the era of big data, processing and visualizing large datasets can be resource-intensive. Techniques like data sampling, aggregation, and interactive visualizations help mitigate these challenges. The choice of visualization techniques demands an understanding of the data's characteristics and the insights sought.

Moreover, EDA requires a balance between depth and efficiency. While delving deep into specific aspects yields rich insights, the need for timely results demands a pragmatic approach. Striking this balance requires experience, domain knowledge, and a discerning eye for patterns that merit further exploration.

Exploratory Data Analysis is a transformative journey that transcends numbers and charts, illuminating the hidden narratives within data. It empowers data scientists to ask questions, unravel patterns, and uncover insights that steer analyses towards meaningful outcomes. As data complexity grows and sources proliferate, the art of EDA remains an essential tool in the data scientist's repertoire.

EDA is not just a technique; it's a mindset that fosters curiosity and critical thinking. It epitomizes the essence of data science—an unceasing quest for knowledge, driven by the desire to unearth insights that drive innovation, understanding, and progress. In this age of information, where data abounds and complexity deepens, EDA stands as a torchbearer, guiding us through the uncharted territories of data, revealing stories that lie beneath the surface, waiting to be discovered.

CHAPTER III

Machine Learning Basics

Introduction to Machine Learning Algorithms

In the era of data-driven decision-making, where the volume of information surpasses human capacity, the advent of machine learning algorithms has ushered in a new era of computational intelligence. Machine learning algorithms, the engines behind predictive modeling, pattern recognition, and automated decision-making, empower systems to learn from data without being explicitly programmed. This section embarks on an exploration of the landscape of machine learning algorithms, elucidating their types, methodologies, and transformative impact on industries ranging from healthcare to finance and beyond.

Machine learning algorithms are at the center of artificial intelligence, bestowing systems with the ability to improve their performance over time through experience. At their essence, these algorithms leverage data to learn patterns, relationships, and rules that enable them to make predictions or decisions without human intervention. Unlike traditional programming, where rules are explicitly defined, machine learning algorithms derive insights from data, iteratively refining their understanding as more information becomes available.

Machine learning algorithms is classified into three fundamental types: supervised, unsupervised, and reinforcement learning. In supervised learning, algorithms learn from labeled data, making predictions or classifications based on patterns learned during training. Unsupervised learning involves analyzing unlabeled data to uncover underlying structures, such as clusters or patterns. Reinforcement learning introduces an element of decision-making, as algorithms learn how to perform actions to maximize rewards based on interactions with an environment.

Within the realm of machine learning, a plethora of algorithms exists, each designed to solve specific types of problems. In supervised learning, linear regression models establish relationships between input variables and continuous output, while decision trees and random forests excel in both classification and regression tasks. Support vector machines and neural networks wield their power in complex pattern recognition tasks.

Unsupervised learning encompasses techniques like K-Means clustering, which groups similar data points, and dimensionality reduction methods like Principal Component Analysis (PCA), which compress data while retaining its essence. Reinforcement learning, on the other hand, finds application in training autonomous agents and robots to make sequential decisions, as exemplified by AlphaGo's mastery of the ancient game of Go.

Machine learning algorithms rely on methodologies that ensure optimal learning and generalization. Data preprocessing, including normalization, scaling, and handling missing values, ensures that input data is suitable for analysis. Feature engineering involves selecting relevant features and transforming them to enhance model performance. Cross-validation techniques validate models on different subsets of data to assess their robustness.

However, challenges persist. Overfitting occurs when models learn training data too well, capturing noise rather than patterns. Regularization techniques mitigate overfitting by adding penalty terms to model parameters. Bias and fairness considerations ensure that models don't perpetuate societal biases present in data. Ethical concerns, like the potential for biased decision-making or invasions of privacy, require rigorous attention.

Machine learning algorithms have permeated diverse industries, transforming the way decisions are made and processes optimized. In healthcare, algorithms diagnose diseases, predict patient outcomes, and aid drug discovery. In finance, predictive models guide investment decisions and detect fraudulent activities. E-commerce platforms employ recommendation systems to personalize user experiences, while autonomous vehicles navigate the streets using machine learning-powered algorithms.

Machine learning algorithms embody the promise of artificial intelligence, equipping systems with the capacity to learn, adapt, and evolve. From the elegance of linear regression to the complexity of deep neural networks, these algorithms span a spectrum of techniques, each offering a unique approach to solving data-driven challenges. The symbiotic relationship between machine learning and data science continues to push the boundaries of what's possible, enabling us to unlock insights, drive innovation, and make informed decisions in a world where data reigns supreme. As the algorithms evolve, one thing remains clear: the transformative potential of machine learning is poised to reshape industries, reshape human experience, and usher in an era of unprecedented computational intelligence.

Supervised, Unsupervised, and Semi-Supervised Learning

In the realm of machine learning, where algorithms are the architects of intelligent systems, the dimensions of learning span a spectrum that encompasses supervised, unsupervised, and semi-supervised paradigms. These paradigms define how machines acquire knowledge from data, each with its distinctive methodologies, applications, and transformative potential. This section embarks on an exploration of these dimensions, shedding light on their nuances, significance, and their impact on diverse domains, from healthcare to finance and beyond.

Supervised learning stands as the cornerstone of machine learning, where algorithms learn from labeled training data to make predictions or classifications on new, unseen data. In this paradigm, the learning process involves mapping input data to desired output labels, enabling algorithms to discern patterns and relationships. Supervised learning is the bedrock of many real-world applications, from predicting stock prices to diagnosing diseases.

Classification and regression are the two primary branches of supervised learning. Classification entails assigning data points to predefined classes, like categorizing emails as spam or not spam. Regression, on the other hand, involves predicting continuous output values, such as estimating the price of a house based on its features. Support vector machines (SVM), decision trees, as well as neural networks are some of the algorithms that thrive in the realm of supervised learning.

Unsupervised learning, in stark contrast to its supervised counterpart, explores the terrain of unlabeled data, where algorithms uncover hidden structures and patterns without predefined output labels. Clustering and dimensionality reduction are the key domains of unsupervised learning. Clustering algorithms group similar data points, revealing natural partitions in the data. This approach has applications in customer segmentation, image segmentation, and more.

Dimensionality reduction techniques like PCA compress high-dimensional data into lower dimensions while preserving its essence. This not only aids in data visualization but also mitigates the curse of dimensionality, where the presence of numerous features can lead to computational challenges and overfitting. Semi-supervised learning strikes a harmonious chord between the labeled and unlabeled realms, leveraging both to enrich the learning process. In this paradigm, limited labeled data is augmented with a larger pool of unlabeled data, harnessing the benefits of supervised learning's precision and unsupervised learning's capacity to uncover patterns. Semi-supervised learning is particularly valuable in scenarios where labeled data is scarce and expensive to acquire.

One notable technique in semi-supervised learning is the incorporation of generative models, such as Generative Adversarial Networks (GANs) and Variational Autoencoders (VAEs). These models generate synthetic data points that align with the distribution of the training data, effectively expanding the labeled dataset and enhancing the performance of supervised learning algorithms.

The dimensions of supervised, unsupervised, and semi-supervised learning reverberate across industries, transforming the landscape of decision-making, automation, and innovation. In healthcare, supervised learning models aid in disease diagnosis, while unsupervised clustering uncovers patient subgroups. In finance, supervised learning algorithms predict market trends, while unsupervised techniques reveal patterns in consumer behavior.

Semi-supervised learning's contribution lies in its potential to democratize machine learning applications. It enables leveraging the vast expanse of unlabeled data that often remains underutilized. Semi-supervised techniques bridge the gap between resource-intensive fully supervised learning and the inherent limitations of unsupervised learning.

Each dimension of learning brings its set of challenges. Supervised learning requires substantial labeled data, which can be expensive and time-consuming to obtain. The success of supervised learning algorithms is contingent on the quality and representativeness of the labeled data. Unsupervised learning, while versatile, can be subjective in interpretation, as patterns and clusters depend on the algorithm's settings and the analyst's perspective.

Semi-supervised learning grapples with the intricacies of balancing labeled and unlabeled data, ensuring that the synthetic data generated align with the distribution of the real data. Evaluating the performance of semi-supervised models also demands careful consideration, as the conventional metrics for supervised learning might not translate seamlessly.

Supervised, unsupervised, and semi-supervised learning constitute the triptych of machine learning dimensions, each imbued with its essence and purpose. These dimensions reflect the myriad ways machines can acquire knowledge from data, from the precision of supervised learning to the exploratory nature of unsupervised learning and the resource efficiency of semi-supervised learning.

The transformative potential of these dimensions is boundless, influencing domains that span from artificial intelligence to scientific discovery. As the boundaries between labeled and unlabeled territories blur, the machine learning landscape evolves, revealing a spectrum of possibilities that reshape how we perceive information, make decisions, and navigate the intricacies of the modern world. In this symphony of algorithms and data, the dimensions of machine learning harmonize, orchestrating a narrative of computational intelligence that unfolds with every data point and prediction, unraveling the secrets of the digital age.

Model Selection and Evaluation Metrics

In the landscape of machine learning, where algorithms hold the key to unlocking patterns and insights within data, the twin pillars of model selection and evaluation metrics stand as sentinels of accuracy and performance. These critical aspects determine the efficacy of machine learning models in making predictions, classifications, and decisions. This section embarks on a journey through the intricacies of model selection and evaluation metrics, uncovering their significance, methodologies, and their transformative role in shaping the landscape of modern data-driven decision-making.

Model selection is akin to navigating a labyrinth of algorithms, searching for the optimal architecture that best captures the patterns within the data. With an array of machine learning algorithms at their disposal—ranging from linear regression and decision trees to support vector machines and neural networks—data scientists face the challenge of selecting the algorithm that will yield the highest accuracy and generalization on unseen data.

The process of model selection encompasses a blend of art and science. It requires understanding the characteristics of the data, the problem at hand, and the strengths and limitations of various algorithms. This iterative exploration involves training multiple models, tuning hyperparameters, and assessing their performance using validation techniques.

Evaluation metrics serve as the yardstick against which the performance of machine learning models is measured. These metrics quantify how well models generalize to new, unseen data. The selection of evaluation metric depends on the type of problem—classification, regression, clustering—and the desired outcomes. A plethora of evaluation metrics exist, each tailored to specific types of analyses.

For classification tasks, metrics including accuracy, precision, F1-score, recall, as well as the area under the receiver operating characteristic curve (AUC-ROC) provide insights into a model's ability to correctly predict classes. In regression tasks, metrics like Mean Squared Error (or MSE), Root Mean Squared Error (or RMSE), and Mean Absolute Error (or MAE) gauge the model's accuracy in predicting continuous values. These evaluation metrics not only facilitate model comparison but also inform model refinement.

The process of model selection is replete with challenges. Overfitting, a common pitfall, occurs when a model learns the training data too well, capturing noise and idiosyncrasies that do not generalize to new data. Cross-validation, a technique used during model selection, mitigates overfitting by dividing the data into subsets for training and validation. Multiple rounds of training and validation help assess a model's performance across different data partitions, revealing its stability and potential for generalization.

Bias in model evaluation is another challenge. If models are evaluated solely on a single dataset, the results might be biased towards the characteristics of that dataset. Cross-validation aids in reducing this bias by assessing models on various subsets of data, ensuring that the model's performance is robust across different scenarios. Machine learning models are defined by hyperparameters—parameters that are not learned from the data but are set by the data scientist. These hyperparameters affect a model's performance and generalization capacity. Hyperparameter tuning is the process of optimizing these parameters to achieve the best model performance.

Hyperparameter tuning involves an intricate dance of exploration and exploitation. Techniques like grid search and random search traverse the hyperparameter space, testing different combinations to identify the optimal configuration. More advanced approaches, such as Bayesian optimization and genetic algorithms, enhance efficiency by leveraging past evaluations to guide the search.

Model selection is inherently tied to the trade-off between bias and variance. The error introduced by approximating a problem in the real-world, which may be complex, with a simplified model, is known as bias. Variance, on the other hand, refers to a model's sensitivity to fluctuations in the training data. The bias-variance trade-off illustrates the delicate balance between fitting a model too close to the training data (overfitting) and not capturing its underlying patterns (underfitting).

Evaluating models through this lens helps data scientists make informed decisions. An overly complex model might perform well on training data but poorly on new data, indicating high variance and potential overfitting. A simple model might exhibit high bias and struggle to capture the complexities of the problem. Model selection involves finding the equilibrium that minimizes both bias and variance.

The repercussions of model selection and evaluation metrics extend far beyond the realm of algorithms. They have transformative implications for real-world decision-making. In fields like healthcare, finance, and marketing, model selection can determine the accuracy of disease diagnoses, investment predictions, and personalized recommendations. Organizations make critical decisions based on the insights extracted from machine learning models, making model selection and evaluation metrics paramount.

Furthermore, model selection influences the deployment of machine learning models in production environments. Scalability, computational resources, and real-time performance considerations play a role in determining which model is not only accurate but also feasible for deployment.

Model selection and evaluation are not devoid of ethical considerations. Biases present in training data can propagate through models, leading to biased predictions and perpetuating inequalities. Responsible model selection involves rigorous examination of the data, proactive measures to identify and mitigate biases, and continuous monitoring of model performance to ensure fair and equitable outcomes.

Model selection and evaluation metrics constitute the compass that guides machine learning journeys, steering them towards the shores of accuracy, reliability, and actionable insights. The art of selecting the right algorithm and fine-tuning its parameters, paired with the science of evaluation metrics, empowers data scientists to harness the potential of data-driven intelligence. In an age where the ramifications of decisions extend beyond human comprehension, the significance of model selection and evaluation metrics emerges as the cornerstone of responsible and transformative AI. As algorithms evolve, datasets expand, and industries embrace the power of machine learning, the fidelity of these twin pillars remains steadfast, guiding the way towards a future illuminated by data-driven knowledge and innovation.

CHAPTER IV

Feature Engineering

Importance of Feature Engineering

In the realm of machine learning, where algorithms are the architects of intelligence, the concept of feature engineering emerges as a hidden gem—a process that transforms raw data into a symphony of insights. Feature engineering, the art and science of selecting, creating, and transforming variables or features to optimize model performance, stands as a pivotal juncture where domain knowledge meets computational prowess. This section embarks on an exploration of the importance of feature engineering, unraveling its significance, methodologies, and its transformative role in shaping the landscape of modern data science.

At its core, feature engineering delves into the notion that data, in its raw form, might not be optimally suited for machine learning. The goal is to transform the data into a format that enables algorithms to extract meaningful patterns and relationships. Features are the building blocks upon which machine learning models construct their understanding of the world. Feature engineering encapsulates the process of selecting relevant features, creating new features, and transforming existing ones.

Feature engineering involves domain expertise, creative thinking, and a deep understanding of the data. It bridges the gap between the intricacies of the real world and the algorithms' capacity to interpret it. Effective feature engineering enables algorithms to recognize patterns that might not be discernible in raw data, enhancing their predictive power and generalization capabilities.

Feature engineering stands as a transformative catalyst in the machine learning journey. Its impact reverberates across every stage, from data preprocessing to model selection and evaluation. Well-engineered features enhance a model's ability to learn complex relationships, thereby improving its accuracy and robustness. Feature engineering can also mitigate the curse of dimensionality, where the presence of numerous features can overwhelm algorithms and lead to overfitting.

In classification tasks, the choice and quality of features can spell the difference between accurate predictions and misclassifications. In regression, well-engineered features can make the distinction between accurate price predictions and wildly inaccurate estimations. The impact of feature engineering extends to natural language processing, computer vision, and other domains, where tailored features enable algorithms to extract semantics and context.

Feature engineering encompasses a spectrum of techniques, each designed to extract certain types of information from the data. Techniques like normalization and scaling ensure that features are on the same scale, preventing certain features from disproportionately influencing the model. Encoding categorical variables, through methods like one-hot encoding, transforms categorical data into numerical format that algorithms can process.

Creating new features is another facet of feature engineering. This involves combining or transforming existing features to capture new information. Domain knowledge plays a pivotal role here, as insights about relationships between features can lead to novel and informative combinations. Feature extraction techniques, like Principal Component Analysis (or PCA) and t-SNE, compress high-dimensional data into lower dimensions while preserving their essence.

The human touch of domain knowledge and creativity in feature engineering is indispensable. Domain experts possess a nuanced understanding of the data's nuances, enabling them to engineer features that encapsulate hidden relationships. For instance, in medical diagnostics, a feature might be engineered to capture the combination of specific symptoms indicative of a disease. In text analysis, features might be designed to capture sentiment, context, or linguistic patterns.

Creativity in feature engineering stems from the ability to view data from different angles, to question assumptions, and to think beyond the obvious. This creative flair often yields features that unlock previously untapped insights, leading to superior model performance.

Feature engineering is not without its challenges. The process requires iterative experimentation, as not all engineered features will enhance model performance. Over-engineering features can lead to the inclusion of noise or introduce multicollinearity, where features are highly correlated. Balancing simplicity and complexity is crucial.

Feature engineering also demands careful consideration of computational resources and time constraints. In the era of big data, processing and engineering features for large datasets can be resource-intensive. Automated feature selection techniques, like recursive feature elimination and L1 regularization, can aid in streamlining the process.

Feature engineering transforms raw data into contextualized knowledge. It enables algorithms to unravel insights that are not explicitly present in the data. It empowers machine learning models to transcend numbers and charts, capturing the essence of the real world they seek to emulate.

Consider a predictive model for housing prices. Raw data might include variables like square footage, number of bedrooms, and location. Feature engineering can enrich this dataset by creating new features like price per square foot, proximity to amenities, and historical market trends. These features encapsulate contextual information that enhances the model's accuracy in predicting housing prices.

Feature engineering stands as a testament to the symbiotic relationship between human expertise and computational power. It merges domain knowledge with algorithmic prowess, elevating machine learning from a mechanical process to an artful journey of discovery. As data complexity grows and industries embrace the potential of machine learning, the importance of feature engineering remains steadfast.

Feature engineering is more than a technical process; it's an act of storytelling. It transforms data points into narratives, uncovering the intricate connections that shape our world. In the symphony of algorithms and data, feature engineering is the conductor that orchestrates meaningful insights, unveiling the latent patterns that lay concealed beneath the surface. As the algorithms evolve and the realm of data science expands, the creative alchemy of feature engineering will continue to define the frontiers of possibility, turning raw data into knowledge, and knowledge into innovation.

Techniques for Feature Extraction and Transformation

In the intricate landscape of feature engineering, where raw data is sculpted into the building blocks of intelligence, the techniques of feature extraction and transformation stand as the artisans of the craft. These techniques wield the power to unearth hidden insights, distill complex relationships, and transform data into a symphony of meaningful features. This section embarks on a journey through the realm of feature extraction and transformation, delving into their methodologies, significance, and their transformative role in shaping the landscape of modern data science.

Feature extraction and transformation are integral to the process of converting raw data into informative features that enhance machine learning model performance. Feature extraction involves deriving new features from existing data by selecting relevant components or patterns. This process reduces the dimensionality of the data while preserving its essence. Feature transformation, on the other hand, involves manipulating or scaling features to enhance their interpretability, distribution, or relationships with other features.

The overarching goal of these techniques is to expose the inherent structure of data, enabling machine learning algorithms to capture patterns that might remain concealed in raw form. Effective feature extraction and transformation equip models with a richer understanding of the data, thereby enhancing their predictive power and generalization capacity.

The significance of feature extraction and transformation extends beyond data preprocessing; it permeates every layer of the machine learning journey. In classification tasks, well-extracted features can unveil subtle patterns that might be crucial for accurate predictions. In regression, transformed features can enhance the model's ability to capture nonlinear relationships, leading to more accurate predictions of continuous variables.

Feature extraction and transformation are particularly relevant in domains where the raw data's complexity might hinder model performance. For instance, in image processing, extracting features like edges, textures, and colors from raw pixel values simplifies the data and allows models to capture visual patterns. In natural language processing, transforming text data into numerical vectors using techniques like TF-IDF or word embeddings enables algorithms to analyze and predict textual content.

Feature extraction techniques span a diverse spectrum, each tailored to capture specific aspects of the data. Principal Component Analysis (PCA) compresses high-dimensional data into lower dimensions while retaining its variance. This technique is particularly valuable when dealing with multicollinearity and the curse of dimensionality. Independent Component Analysis (ICA) identifies underlying independent sources within mixed data, aiding in signal separation.

For text data, techniques like Term Frequency-Inverse Document Frequency (TF-IDF) quantify the importance of words in documents, facilitating sentiment analysis and document clustering. In computer vision, Convolutional Neural Networks (CNNs) automatically extract hierarchical features from images, enabling object detection, classification, and image generation.

Feature transformation techniques enhance features' quality, distribution, and relationships. Scaling techniques like Min-Max Scaling and Standardization normalize features to specific ranges, preventing features with larger magnitudes from dominating the analysis. Logarithmic and power transformations modify feature distributions, enabling algorithms to capture nonlinear relationships.

Polynomial features, generated by squaring or multiplying existing features, introduce polynomial relationships into the model. This is particularly useful when linear relationships do not suffice in capturing the complexity of the data. Interaction terms, which represent combinations of two or more features, provide insights into synergistic relationships between variables.

Feature extraction and transformation are not one-size-fits-all processes; they require tailoring to specific domains and problems. In the field of genetics, where DNA sequences are analyzed, features might involve codon frequencies, GC content, and secondary structures. In finance, where time series data prevails, features might include moving averages, volatility measures, and technical indicators.

Domain expertise plays a pivotal role in selecting the right extraction and transformation techniques. It empowers data scientists to make informed decisions about which features are relevant, what relationships might exist, and how transformed features align with the problem's context.

Feature extraction and transformation are not without challenges. Over-engineering features can lead to overfitting, where models learn noise rather than patterns. Striking the balance between feature richness and model simplicity is crucial. Moreover, some techniques are computationally expensive, making them less feasible for large datasets or real-time applications.

Feature transformation can also introduce multicollinearity, where transformed features are highly correlated. This can hinder model interpretability and lead to unstable coefficients. Techniques like Variance Inflation Factor (VIF) can help identify and mitigate multicollinearity by quantifying the extent to which features are linearly dependent on others.

Feature extraction and transformation aren't devoid of ethical considerations. Biases present in data can propagate through extracted or transformed features, leading to biased model predictions. Responsible feature engineering demands scrutiny of the data, proactive measures to identify and address biases, and continuous monitoring of feature performance.

Feature extraction and transformation are the artisans of feature engineering, revealing the artistry hidden within data. These techniques empower machine learning algorithms to perceive patterns, relationships, and trends that might elude raw data. The journey from raw data to meaningful insights is orchestrated by the transformative power of feature extraction and transformation.

In an age where data complexity burgeons and industries embrace the potential of machine learning, the significance of these techniques remains unwavering. They infuse data with context, breathe life into numbers, and empower algorithms to uncover truths. As the frontiers of data science continue to expand and algorithms evolve, the techniques of feature extraction and transformation will continue to shape the landscape of intelligence, turning data into knowledge and knowledge into innovation.

Dealing with Missing Data and Outliers

In the vast sea of data that fuels the engine of machine learning, the challenges of missing data and outliers emerge as tumultuous waves, threatening to distort the integrity of insights. Addressing these challenges through strategic techniques within feature engineering is not just a requisite for accurate predictions, but a testament to the artistry of data science. This section embarks on a voyage through the realms of missing data and outliers, unveiling their significance, methodologies, and their transformative role in shaping the seascape of modern data analysis.

Missing data are gaps in a dataset where values should ideally be present. These gaps might arise due to various reasons, such as measurement errors, survey non-responses, or system failures. Outliers, on the other hand, are observations that deviate significantly from the norm or the bulk of the data. They can stem from genuine anomalies, data collection errors, or natural variability.

Missing data and outliers have the potential to skew analyses, mislead interpretations, and hinder the performance of machine learning models. Addressing these challenges within feature engineering is imperative to ensure accurate, reliable, and meaningful outcomes.

The impact of missing data is far-reaching. It can result in biased results, as the analysis might be based on an incomplete or non-representative sample. Missing data can also introduce inefficiencies in model training, as algorithms struggle to interpret gaps in information. In predictive modeling, missing data can severely affect the accuracy of predictions, as models trained on incomplete data might generalize poorly to new data.

Addressing missing data is not just about filling gaps; it's about preserving the data's integrity and ensuring that analyses are grounded in reality. The techniques employed must consider the reasons for missingness, the potential bias introduced, and the implications for downstream analyses.

Imputation is a key technique for handling missing data. It involves filling in missing values using various methods. Simple imputation techniques like mean, median, or mode imputation replace missing values with the mean, median, or mode of the feature. These methods are useful when missing data is missing completely at random (or MCAR) or missing at random (or MAR).

For more sophisticated imputation, predictive modeling techniques can be employed. Linear regression, decision trees, or even more complex models can predict missing values based on other features. Multiple imputation involves creating multiple imputed datasets and combining their results, accounting for the uncertainty introduced by missing data.

Outliers, as data points that diverge from the norm, can significantly impact analysis results. They might distort statistical summaries, affect parameter estimates, and lead to poor model generalization. However, not all outliers are errors; some may represent legitimate observations or rare events.

The approach to handling outliers depends on the domain and the context of the analysis. In some cases, outliers might be removed if they are deemed data errors. In others, they might be transformed or winsorized (capped at a certain value) to reduce their impact. Robust statistical techniques, like the Median Absolute Deviation (MAD) or the Huber loss function, can be employed to mitigate the influence of outliers on parameter estimates.

Outlier detection techniques aim to identify and isolate potential outliers. Z-score normalization calculates how far each data point is from the mean in terms of standard deviations. Data points that fall beyond a certain threshold are flagged as potential outliers. Box plots visualize the distribution of data and identify outliers beyond the whiskers.

Clustering techniques like k-means can identify clusters of similar data points. Data points that do not belong to any cluster might be potential outliers. Machine learning algorithms like Isolation Forests and Local Outlier Factor (LOF) score data points based on their isolation or local density, respectively.

The strategies for handling missing data and outliers are not universally applicable. They require consideration of the nature of the data, the problem at hand, and the potential consequences of the chosen approach. Imputing missing values should be done with care, considering the implications for downstream analyses and potential bias introduced.

Outliers might be valuable in certain contexts. For example, in fraud detection, outliers might represent fraudulent transactions. Thus, blindly removing all outliers might lead to loss of critical information. The chosen technique should align with the problem's objectives and the data's characteristics.

Addressing missing data and outliers has ethical implications. Removing or imputing data can impact the integrity of the analysis and potentially introduce biases. Careful consideration of the causes for missing data and the potential consequences of handling techniques is crucial.

Dealing with missing data and outliers is a nuanced art that requires a combination of domain expertise, statistical knowledge, and computational prowess. These challenges are not mere obstacles; they are opportunities to refine data quality and uncover hidden insights. In the evolving landscape of data science, the ability to adeptly address missing data and outliers is not just a technical skill; it's a testament to the artistry of data exploration.

As industries embrace the potential of data-driven decision-making, the significance of handling missing data and outliers remains unwavering. These challenges might be tempestuous waters, but they are navigable with the right techniques and a steadfast commitment to data quality. The voyage from raw data to meaningful insights is guided by the transformative power of addressing missing data and outliers, shaping the seascape of data-driven intelligence, and illuminating the path to accurate, informed, and responsible decisions.

CHAPTER V

Supervised Learning Algorithms

Linear Regression

In the symphony of supervised learning algorithms, where data orchestrates the composition and algorithms perform the melody, linear regression emerges as a foundational note—a powerful and elegant tool that underpins predictive modeling. This section embarks on a journey through the intricacies of linear regression, exploring its essence, methodologies, significance, and its transformative role in shaping the landscape of modern data-driven decision-making.

Fundamentally, linear regression is a statistical method that fits a linear equation to observed data to represent the connection between a dependent variable (goal) and one or more independent variables (features). Finding the best-fitting line that reduces the difference between the expected and actual values is the aim. Linear regression aims to capture the underlying trend and quantify the relationship between variables, enabling predictions and inference.

Linear regression is not only a tool for predictive modeling but also a lens through which relationships between variables can be understood and interpreted. Its simplicity and interpretability make it a cornerstone in various fields, from economics and finance to biology and social sciences.

Linear regression holds a special place in the supervised learning repertoire due to its versatility and interpretability. It is a building block for more complex algorithms and models. Understanding linear regression provides a solid foundation for comprehending more advanced techniques, such as ridge regression, LASSO regression, and generalized linear models.

Moreover, linear regression provides insights beyond predictions. The coefficients of the linear equation offer quantitative information about the strength and direction of connections between variables. This interpretability is crucial in fields where the goal is not only prediction but also understanding the underlying dynamics, such as in medical research, where identifying risk factors is as important as predicting outcomes.

The methodology of linear regression involves finding the optimal coefficients for the linear equation that best fits the data. This is achieved through the process of Ordinary Least Squares (OLS) optimization, which reduces the sum of the squared differences between the forecasted values and actual values. The OLS method seeks to find the line that minimizes the vertical distances between data points and the line.

Linear regression can be univariate, involving a single independent variable, or multivariate, incorporating multiple independent variables. In multivariate regression, the relationship between the dependent variable and each independent variable is isolated, controlling for the effects of other variables.

Linear regression comes with assumptions that need to be met for the results to be valid. The assumptions include linearity, independence, homoscedasticity (constant variance of residuals), and normally distributed residuals. Violations of these hypothesis can lead to biased or unreliable results.

Addressing these challenges often involves data preprocessing, transformation, and robust statistical techniques. Feature engineering, outlier detection, and validation methods like cross-validation play a role in enhancing the performance and reliability of linear regression models.

Linear regression is not confined to simple straight-line relationships. Polynomial regression extends the linear model to capture nonlinear relationships by adding polynomial terms. Regularized regression techniques like ridge regression and LASSO introduce penalty terms that prevent overfitting and lead to more stable coefficients. In multiple linear regression, interactions between variables can be explored by including interaction terms.

This enables the model to capture how the relationship between variables changes based on different conditions. The applications of linear regression are diverse and span industries. In economics, linear regression models predict factors like GDP growth based on variables such as inflation rates and interest rates. In healthcare, linear regression helps predict disease progression based on biomarkers. In marketing, it aids in predicting consumer behavior based on demographic and behavioral variables.

Linear regression's significance extends beyond prediction; it contributes to decision-making and policy formulation. For instance, by understanding the relationship between advertising expenditures and sales, companies can optimize their marketing budgets. Linear regression's insights shape strategies, guide resource allocation, and drive informed actions.

Linear regression, like all algorithms, is not immune to biases present in the data. Biases can lead to inaccurate predictions and reinforce inequalities. Responsible use of linear regression involves meticulous examination of the data, detection and mitigation of biases, and continuous monitoring of the model's performance.

Linear regression, as one of the cornerstones of supervised learning, exemplifies the synergy between mathematics, statistics, and real-world insights. Its elegance lies not just in its mathematical formulation but in its capacity to reveal relationships, predict outcomes, and guide decisions. In an era of complex algorithms and sprawling datasets, linear regression stands as a reminder of the enduring value of simplicity and interpretability.

As industries traverse the landscape of data-driven decision-making, linear regression remains a constant, adapting and evolving to meet the challenges of changing times. Its legacy is etched in the foundations of predictive modeling, providing a bridge between data and actionable insights. In this intricate dance of data and algorithms, linear regression's melody resonates—an ode to the power of understanding, a testament to the synergy of variables, and a symphony of knowledge that continues to shape the future of intelligence.

Logistic Regression

In the realm of supervised learning, where algorithms navigate the terrain of data to make predictions and decisions, logistic regression emerges as a beacon—a versatile and powerful tool that seamlessly bridges the worlds of classification and probability. This section embarks on a journey through the intricacies of logistic regression, exploring its essence, methodologies, significance, and its transformative role in shaping the landscape of modern data-driven decision-making.

Logistic regression is a statistical technique that extends the principles of linear regression to the domain of classification. Unlike linear regression, which predicts continuous outcomes, logistic regression predicts the probability of an instance belonging to a particular class. This makes logistic regression particularly well-suited for binary classification tasks, where the objective is to assign instances to one of two classes.

The core concept behind logistic regression lies in the logistic function, or the sigmoid function. This function transforms the output of a linear equation into a value between 0 and 1, showing the probability of an instance belonging to a specific class. The logistic function's S-shaped curve is instrumental in mapping the linear combination of features to probabilities.

Logistic regression's significance extends beyond its utility in classification tasks. Its outputs—probabilities—align seamlessly with the language of uncertainty and probability theory. This aligns with the inherent uncertainty in many real-world decisions, where predictions are rarely absolute but rather nuanced by probabilities.

Moreover, the simplicity and interpretability of logistic regression make it an indispensable tool. The coefficients of the model's equation offer insights into the relationships between features and the log-odds of the outcome. This interpretability enables domain experts to grasp the logic behind predictions and fosters understanding, transparency, and trust.

The methodology of logistic regression involves finding the optimal coefficients that best fit the data and maximize the likelihood of the observed outcomes. The logistic function converts the linear combination of features and coefficients into probabilities. The model's parameters are usually estimated through techniques like Maximum Likelihood Estimation (MLE).

Regularization techniques, such as L1 regularization (LASSO) and L2 regularization (ridge), can be applied to mitigate overfitting and enhance the model's generalization capacity. These techniques introduce penalty terms that constrain the magnitude of coefficients, preventing them from becoming too large.

Logistic regression is not without challenges. The model assumes linearity between features and the log-odds of the outcome. Deviations from linearity can lead to poor model fit and biased predictions. Feature engineering, interactions, and transformations play a role in addressing this challenge.

Moreover, class imbalance, where one class is much more prevalent than the other, can lead to biased models that favor the majority class. Techniques like oversampling, undersampling, and Synthetic Minority Over-sampling Technique (SMOTE) help balance class distribution and improve model performance.

Logistic regression is not confined to binary classification. Multinomial logistic regression handles cases where there are more than two classes, assigning probabilities to each class. Ordinal logistic regression is employed when the classes have a natural order, predicting the likelihood of an instance belonging to a certain ordinal class.

Logistic regression can also be extended to handle more complex relationships between features and the outcome. Polynomial logistic regression introduces polynomial terms to capture nonlinear relationships. Interaction terms can represent synergistic or antagonistic relationships between features.

The applications of logistic regression are wide-ranging. In medicine, it aids in predicting disease outcomes based on patient characteristics. In finance, it assesses credit risk by predicting the likelihood of default. In marketing, it models customer behavior to guide targeted campaigns.

Logistic regression's value extends beyond prediction. Its outputs—probabilities—can inform decision-making by quantifying uncertainty. For instance, in healthcare, predicting the probability of disease recurrence guides treatment strategies. In criminal justice, predicting the likelihood of recidivism informs parole decisions.

Like all algorithms, logistic regression must be wielded responsibly. Biases present in the data can lead to biased predictions, potentially perpetuating inequalities. Responsible use involves continuous monitoring, bias detection, and mitigation strategies to ensure fairness and equity.

Logistic regression's significance lies not just in its predictive prowess, but in its ability to elegantly blend the worlds of classification and probability. It exemplifies the power of harnessing uncertainty and quantifying ambiguity—a key aspect of real-world decision-making. In an era of sophisticated algorithms and complex data landscapes, logistic regression stands as a reminder of the enduring value of simplicity and interpretability.

As industries embrace the potential of data-driven decisions, logistic regression remains a steadfast companion, adapting and evolving to meet the difficulties of changing times. Its legacy is etched in the foundations of classification and probability, providing a bridge between the certainty of classification and the nuance of probability. In this intricate dance of data and algorithms, logistic regression's rhythm resonates—an ode to the synergy of features, a testament to the power of probability, and a symphony of informed choices that continue to shape the future of intelligence.

Decision Trees and Random Forests

In the vast expanse of supervised learning, where algorithms traverse the landscapes of data to uncover patterns and make predictions, decision trees and their formidable offspring, random forests, emerge as towering sentinels—an embodiment of the elegance and strength of ensemble learning. This section embarks on a journey through the intricacies of decision trees and random forests, delving into their essence, methodologies, significance, and their transformative role in shaping the landscape of modern data-driven decision-making.

A decision tree is a hierarchical framework that divides data into subsets recursively according to the values of input attributes in order to facilitate decision-making. Every internal node indicates a choice made in response to a certain characteristic, which results in nodes or leaves that represent expected consequences in the future. The decision-making process that leads from a root node to a leaf node finally determines the expected class or value.

Decision trees harness the power of binary logic to map the decision space and categorize instances into classes or predict values. They excel at handling both categorical and numerical features, making them versatile tools for classification and regression tasks.

Decision trees hold significance in their simplicity, interpretability, and adaptability. Their structure aligns with human decision-making processes, making them easy to grasp even for non-experts. Decision trees provide transparent insights into the decision process, enabling users to understand the rationale behind predictions.

Moreover, decision trees offer insights into feature importance. The hierarchy of decisions can highlight which features have the greatest impact on the outcome. This not only aids in model interpretation but also guides feature selection and engineering.

The methodology of decision trees involves recursively selecting features and splitting data to optimize certain criteria. The Gini impurity and entropy are two common measures that assess the purity of subsets created by splits. The goal is to minimize impurity and maximize homogeneity within each subset.

The challenge lies in preventing overfitting, where the tree becomes overly complex and captures noise in the data. Pruning, a technique that removes branches with weak predictive power, helps combat overfitting. Techniques like minimum samples per leaf, maximum depth, and minimum impurity decrease the complexity of the tree.

Decision trees can suffer from high variance and instability, making them sensitive to minor variations in the data. This can lead to poor generalization and unreliable predictions. Techniques like bagging, boosting, and random forests address these challenges through ensemble learning.

Additionally, decision trees can be biased towards features with more categories or levels. This can lead to erroneous decisions based on the prevalence of certain categories. One-hot encoding, weight adjustments, and regularization can mitigate this bias.

An ensemble learning method called random forests makes use of the advantages of several decision trees. By using feature randomization and bootstrapped sampling, random forests generate many decision trees as opposed to depending on a single one. Each tree makes independent predictions, and the final prediction is determined through aggregation, often by majority vote (classification) or averaging (regression).

Random forests mitigate the overfitting problem associated with individual decision trees. The variance introduced by individual trees is reduced through the wisdom of crowds, leading to improved generalization performance and robustness.

Random forests offer a host of advantages that extend beyond decision trees. They are less prone to overfitting due to their ensemble nature, making them suitable for complex datasets. They are also less sensitive to small variations in the data, enhancing stability and reliability.

Random forests are resilient to outliers, as the impact of individual trees is dampened by the aggregation process. This makes them well-suited for noisy or heterogeneous datasets. Moreover, they handle high-dimensional data gracefully, as they consider subsets of features in each tree.

Decision trees and random forests find applications across domains. In healthcare, decision trees can predict disease outcomes based on patient characteristics. In finance, random forests can model credit risk by aggregating the insights of multiple trees. In image processing, decision trees can classify objects based on pixel values.

Random forests extend their prowess to diverse fields. In astronomy, they identify celestial objects from noisy signals. In marketing, they segment customers for targeted campaigns. In ecology, they predict species distribution based on environmental variables.

Ensemble methods like random forests are not immune to biases present in the data. Aggregating biased decisions from multiple trees can amplify these biases. Responsible use involves bias detection, bias mitigation, and ongoing monitoring of model performance.

Decision trees and random forests epitomize the power of ensemble learning—a testament to the fact that the collective wisdom of multiple models is often more powerful than a single model's insight. Their elegance lies in their ability to navigate complex decision spaces, uncover patterns, and generate predictions with enhanced accuracy and robustness.

As industries navigate the ocean of data, decision trees and random forests remain steadfast companions, adapting and evolving to meet the requirements of modern data-driven decision-making. Their legacy is etched in the ensemble's strength, offering a bridge between simplicity and complexity. In this intricate interplay of data and algorithms, decision trees and random forests stand as guardians—a testament to the artistry of aggregation, a symbol of collective intelligence, and a symphony of predictive might that continues to shape the future of intelligence.

Support Vector Machines (SVM)

In the realm of supervised learning, where algorithms endeavor to uncover patterns and make accurate predictions, Support Vector Machines (SVM) emerge as a beacon of geometric elegance—a formidable tool that transcends traditional linear boundaries and extends its reach to intricate decision landscapes. This section embarks on a journey through the intricacies of Support Vector Machines, exploring their essence, methodologies, significance, and their transformative role in shaping the landscape of modern data-driven decision-making.

Support Vector Machines (SVM) are a class of supervised learning algorithms that excel in both classification and regression tasks. At the heart of SVM's power lies its ability to transform data into higher-dimensional spaces, thereby uncovering complex relationships that might be hidden in the original feature space. SVM is particularly known for its prowess in handling high-dimensional data and datasets with separability issues.

The essence of SVM lies in finding a hyperplane that best separates instances belonging to different classes while maximizing the margin between them. This hyperplane is defined by support vectors—data points that are crucial for determining the optimal separating boundary.

SVM's significance extends beyond its classification prowess. Its geometric underpinnings make it capable of capturing nonlinear relationships through the use of kernel functions, thereby extending its utility to a wide array of data distributions. SVM's emphasis on maximizing the margin between classes ensures robust generalization to unseen data, making it a stalwart for high-performance models.

Moreover, SVM's effectiveness in handling high-dimensional data is particularly valuable in the era of big data and complex datasets. Its ability to identify patterns in high-dimensional spaces elevates its position as a versatile tool that adapts to the challenges of modern data analysis.

The methodology of SVM revolves around finding the hyperplane that separates classes while maximizing the margin between them. This is achieved through the optimization of a convex quadratic programming problem. The soft-margin SVM relaxes the constraint for perfect separation to accommodate instances that might lie within the margin or on the wrong side of the hyperplane.

In situations where data is not linearly separable, SVM employs kernel functions to transform the feature space. These functions map the data into a higher-dimensional space where linear separation is possible. Common kernel functions include polynomial kernels, radial basis function (RBF) kernels, and sigmoid kernels.

SVM is not without challenges. The selection of appropriate kernel functions and hyperparameters can impact model performance. An improper choice can lead to overfitting or underfitting. Cross-validation, grid search, and model selection techniques play a role in mitigating these challenges.

Additionally, SVM's scalability can be a concern for large datasets. Training time and memory requirements can increase significantly with the number of instances and features. Techniques like stochastic gradient descent, sequential minimal optimization, and parallel processing can alleviate these scalability issues.

Support Vector Machines find applications in diverse domains. In image classification, SVM can categorize objects based on pixel values. In bioinformatics, SVM aids in protein structure prediction. In finance, SVM models credit risk based on historical data. In text classification, SVM distinguishes between spam and non-spam emails.

SVM's strength extends to domains that require a balance between interpretability and complexity. In medical diagnosis, SVM can predict disease outcomes based on patient data. In sentiment analysis, SVM detects the sentiment expressed in textual content. In face recognition, SVM identifies individuals based on facial features.

SVM's potential for high accuracy and complexity comes with ethical considerations. The model's decisions might be opaque and hard to interpret, leading to the potential for biased predictions. Responsible use involves model validation, fairness audits, and bias detection techniques to ensure that SVM's predictions align with ethical and societal norms.

Support Vector Machines stand as a testament to the power of geometry and optimization in the realm of supervised learning. Their ability to sculpt decision landscapes, transform data into higher-dimensional spaces, and capture intricate patterns sets them apart as an essential tool in the modern data scientist's toolkit.

As industries delve deeper into the ocean of data, Support Vector Machines remain steadfast companions, adapting and evolving to meet the requirements of modern data-driven decision-making. Their legacy is etched in their geometric elegance—a bridge between linear and nonlinear boundaries, a symbol of accuracy, and a symphony of transformation that continues to shape the future of intelligence.

CHAPTER VI

Unsupervised Learning Algorithms

Clustering Techniques (K-Means, Hierarchical Clustering)

In the realm of unsupervised learning, where algorithms delve into the untamed terrain of data to unveil hidden structures and relationships, clustering techniques rise as the compass guiding this exploration—a versatile set of tools that aim to partition data into meaningful groups. This section embarks on a journey through the intricacies of clustering techniques, focusing on K-Means and Hierarchical Clustering, unraveling their essence, methodologies, significance, and their transformative role in shaping the landscape of modern data-driven exploration.

Clustering techniques are at the heart of unsupervised learning, tasked with identifying natural groupings within datasets. Unlike supervised learning, where the algorithm is provided with labeled data, clustering operates on unlabeled data—without prior information about the class labels or categories. The goal is to discover inherent patterns, associations, or similarities among instances.

K-Means and Hierarchical Clustering are two prominent methods within the clustering realm. They strive to identify structures in data, but they approach this task with distinct methodologies, offering varying levels of granularity and insight.

The significance of clustering techniques transcends their role in grouping data. They provide a lens through which data's underlying organization is revealed, allowing data scientists to derive insights, discover anomalies, and gain a deeper understanding of complex datasets. These techniques are pivotal in exploratory data analysis, data preprocessing, customer segmentation, anomaly detection, and more.

Moreover, clustering techniques lay the foundation for downstream tasks like classification and recommendation systems. By grouping similar instances, clustering aids in constructing more accurate models and making personalized recommendations. It serves as a stepping stone in the journey from raw data to actionable insights.

Data is divided into K clusters using the centroid-based clustering technique K-Means. Each cluster is represented by its centroid, which is a point that reduces the sum of squared distances to all of the data points in that cluster. The process begins by initializing K centroids. Next, data points are iteratively assigned to the closest centroid, and the centroids are updated in light of the newly formed clusters.

K-Means optimization involves finding the centroids that minimize the within-cluster variance. It converges to a local optimum, making initialization crucial. Multiple random initializations and the use of techniques like K-Means++ aim to mitigate the impact of suboptimal initial centroids.

Hierarchical Clustering builds a tree-like structure, or dendrogram, that represents the relationships between instances in a hierarchical manner. This approach does not require a predefined number of clusters, allowing for a flexible exploration of different cluster counts. The algorithm starts with each instance as a separate cluster and iteratively merges clusters based on similarity until a single cluster remains.

Agglomerative and divisive are the two main approaches in hierarchical clustering. Agglomerative clustering starts with individual instances and merges them into larger clusters, while divisive clustering starts with all instances as one cluster and divides them into smaller clusters.

Clustering techniques face challenges like determining the optimal number of clusters (K) and handling outliers. In K-Means, choosing an appropriate value for K is a key decision that influences the results. Techniques like the elbow method and silhouette analysis aid in making this choice. Outliers can significantly affect the formation of clusters, leading to imbalanced or distorted groupings.

Hierarchical Clustering's challenge lies in the dendrogram's interpretation and deciding the optimal level of hierarchy to extract clusters. This requires balancing granularity and interpretability. Additionally, hierarchical clustering can be computationally intensive for large datasets due to its quadratic time complexity.

Clustering techniques find applications in various fields. In marketing, customer segmentation helps tailor marketing strategies to different groups. In biology, clustering aids in gene expression analysis to identify functional relationships among genes. In finance, anomaly detection identifies fraudulent transactions.

The transformative potential of clustering extends to diverse domains. In social network analysis, clustering uncovers communities within networks. In image segmentation, clustering identifies distinct regions in images. In natural language processing, clustering groups similar documents for topic modeling.

Ethical considerations in clustering revolve around the interpretation of results and potential bias. Clustering outcomes might inadvertently reinforce stereotypes or groupings that perpetuate inequalities. Careful analysis, validation, and domain expertise are essential to ensure that the extracted clusters align with ethical standards.

Clustering techniques stand as the unsupervised explorers of the data universe, uncovering patterns and relationships that might have remained hidden. Their elegance lies in their ability to transform unlabeled data into insights, guiding data scientists in their quest for understanding and discovery.

As industries navigate the complexities of data, clustering techniques remain invaluable companions, adapting and evolving to meet the challenges of modern data-driven exploration. Their legacy is etched in the divisions and connections they unveil—a bridge between data and insight, a testament to the power of similarity, and a symphony of pattern recognition that continues to shape the future of intelligence.

Dimensionality Reduction (Principal Component Analysis, t-SNE)

In the expansive realm of unsupervised learning, where algorithms navigate the intricate maze of data to discover patterns and uncover insights, dimensionality reduction techniques emerge as guiding stars—powerful tools that aim to simplify complex data spaces while preserving their essence. This section embarks on a journey through the intricacies of dimensionality reduction, focusing on

Principal Component Analysis (PCA) and t-SNE, unraveling their essence, methodologies, significance, and their transformative role in shaping the landscape of modern data-driven exploration.

Dimensionality reduction is a cornerstone of unsupervised learning, designed to address the curse of dimensionality—the inherent challenges posed by high-dimensional data spaces. As data accumulates across numerous dimensions, the risk of noise, redundancy, and computational complexity escalates. Dimensionality reduction techniques aim to distill the meaningful information from the noise, allowing for a more compact representation of data that retains its essential features.

Principal Component Analysis and t-SNE are two pivotal methods within the dimensionality reduction domain. They delve into the realm of data representation, albeit with distinct philosophies and methodologies.

The significance of dimensionality reduction reverberates across the data analysis landscape. It not only simplifies data visualization and comprehension but also contributes to the enhancement of model performance. By reducing the quantity of features, dimensionality reduction techniques help combat overfitting, improve computational efficiency, and provide a streamlined basis for subsequent analysis.

Moreover, dimensionality reduction unlocks hidden insights within data. By transforming data into lower-dimensional spaces, these techniques highlight relationships, trends, and clusters that might have been obscured by the noise inherent in high-dimensional spaces. This serves as a catalyst for exploratory analysis, anomaly detection, and data-driven decision-making.

Principal Component Analysis (or PCA) is a linear dimensionality reduction technique that aims to identify the orthogonal axes (principal components) along which the variance in data is maximized. The first or initial principal component captures the most significant variance, followed by subsequent components in decreasing order of variance. These principal components, which are the linear combination of the original features, define the new feature space.

Eigendecomposition, also known as singular value decomposition, of the data's covariance matrix forms the basis of PCA. This matrix captures the relationships between features, allowing PCA to determine the axes of maximal variance.

t-Distributed Stochastic Neighbor Embedding (or t-SNE) is a nonlinear dimensionality reduction technique renowned for its prowess in visualizing high-dimensional data in lower-dimensional spaces. Unlike PCA, t-SNE's focus is on preserving the pairwise similarities between data points in both the original and reduced spaces. It achieves this by mapping high-dimensional similarities to lower-dimensional similarities, using a probability distribution that is iteratively adjusted to minimize the divergence between these similarities.

t-SNE's iterative nature, along with its emphasis on pairwise relationships, results in a representation where similar instances are clustered together, often revealing intricate structures and relationships within data. This makes t-SNE particularly suited for visualization purposes.

Dimensionality reduction techniques face challenges like information loss and interpretation. While reducing dimensions simplifies data, it might lead to the loss of some nuanced information. The trade-off between simplification and preservation of essential information is a constant consideration.

Furthermore, interpretation of reduced dimensions can be challenging, especially when nonlinear transformations are involved. Translating lower-dimensional representations back to the original feature space might not yield immediately interpretable results. Careful consideration of the transformed data's meaning is crucial.

Dimensionality reduction techniques find applications in various domains. In bioinformatics, PCA aids in analyzing gene expression data. In image analysis, t-SNE unveils clusters of visually similar images. In text mining, PCA aids in topic modeling by simplifying the space of term-document relationships.

The transformative potential of dimensionality reduction extends to fields demanding visualization and insight extraction. In genetics, PCA visualizes genetic variations among populations. In facial recognition, t-SNE clusters similar facial expressions for model training. In customer segmentation, PCA and t-SNE distill complex customer behaviors into interpretable groups.

Ethical considerations in dimensionality reduction center around preserving essential features and avoiding bias. The transformation process might inadvertently remove critical information, leading to misinterpretations or biased insights. Responsible application involves careful validation, domain expertise, and continuous assessment of the transformed data's fidelity.

Dimensionality reduction stands as a beacon in the tumultuous sea of high-dimensional data. Its elegance lies in its ability to peel away layers of complexity while revealing the core essence of information. As industries navigate the labyrinth of data, dimensionality reduction techniques remain indispensable companions, adapting and evolving to meet the challenges of modern data-driven exploration. Their legacy is etched in the unveiling of patterns, the simplification of complexity, and the symphony of representation that continues to shape the future of intelligence.

CHAPTER VII

Neural Networks and Deep Learning

Introduction to Neural Networks

In the vast landscape of artificial intelligence, where algorithms strive to mimic human cognition and learning, neural networks emerge as the bedrock—the cornerstone upon which the edifice of modern AI is constructed. This section embarks on a journey through the intricate tapestry of neural networks, unraveling their essence, methodologies, significance, and their transformative role in shaping the landscape of contemporary data-driven solutions.

Neural networks are the culmination of the quest to replicate the intricate workings of the human brain within the digital realm. At their core, they consist of interconnected nodes, or "neurons," organized in layers. Each neuron processes information, performs computations, and passes signals to subsequent layers, ultimately generating an output. The architecture of neural networks mimics the synaptic connections between neurons in the brain.

The foundation of neural networks is the concept of "deep learning," wherein multiple hidden layers enable the network to learn hierarchical features from data. This capacity to extract increasingly abstract and complex representations is what sets neural networks apart in the field of artificial intelligence.

Neural networks have revolutionized the AI landscape, propelling it into realms previously deemed unattainable. Their ability to learn from extensive amounts of data, adapt to new information, and generalize to unseen instances has given rise to applications spanning various domains. Neural networks have shown unmatched capabilities in a variety of fields, including autonomous driving, natural language processing (NLP), image and speech recognition, and more.

Moreover, neural networks' ability to process unstructured data, like images, text, and audio, has ushered in a new era of data-driven decision-making. They hold the potential to uncover hidden patterns, infer context, and make predictions with a level of accuracy that was once a distant aspiration.

The methodology of neural networks is a symphony of interconnected computations. Input data is passed through layers of neurons, each neuron applying a weighted sum of inputs and applying an activation function. The network iteratively adjusts these weights during training, using backpropagation—
an algorithm that determines the loss function's gradient in relation to each weight. The gradient guides weight updates, gradually refining the network's ability to make accurate predictions.

Neural network architectures vary widely, from the fundamental feedforward networks to more complex structures like convolutional neural networks (or CNNs) for image processing, recurrent neural networks (or RNNs) for sequential data, and transformers for natural language understanding.

Neural networks bring with them a set of challenges and considerations. Training neural networks demands significant computational resources and data, which can make them computationally expensive and resource-intensive. Overfitting—when a model learns to perform well on the training data but fails to generalize to new data—is another challenge, necessitating techniques like dropout and regularization.

Hyperparameter tuning, the process of finding optimal parameter values, is crucial to neural network performance. Selecting the appropriate number of layers, neurons, and activation functions demands experimentation and an understanding of the data at hand.

Neural networks' applications span industries. In healthcare, they aid in disease diagnosis from medical images. In finance, they predict market trends and manage risk. In entertainment, they enable facial recognition for unlocking devices. In language translation, they decode context and semantics for accurate communication.

The transformative potential of neural networks extends across domains. In robotics, they guide autonomous vehicles. In scientific research, they model complex systems and simulate scenarios. In drug discovery, they predict molecular interactions.

With great power comes great responsibility. Neural networks' transformative potential comes with ethical considerations. Models trained on biased data might perpetuate inequalities. Responsible use involves continuous monitoring, bias detection, and mitigation strategies to ensure fairness and transparency.

Neural networks stand as a testament to humanity's quest to unlock the mysteries of intelligence and cognition. Their elegance lies in their ability to learn, adapt, and mimic human thought processes. As industries delve into the ocean of data, neural networks remain steadfast companions, adapting and evolving to meet the challenges of modern data-driven solutions. Their legacy is etched in their capacity to decipher patterns, their role in the AI renaissance, and the symphony of interconnected computations that continues to shape the future of intelligence.

Building Blocks of Neural Networks (Layers, Activation Functions)

In the realm of artificial intelligence, where algorithms strive to replicate human-like learning and cognition, neural networks stand as towering edifices—the epitome of modern AI. Central to the architecture and operation of neural networks are their fundamental building blocks: layers and activation functions. This section embarks on an exploration of these intricate components, delving into their essence, methodologies, significance, and their transformative role in shaping the landscape of contemporary data-driven solutions.

Layers form the backbone of neural networks, akin to the layers of abstraction within human cognition. Each layer is a collection of interconnected neurons, acting as information processing units. Neural networks comprise three main types of layers: input, hidden, and output. The

input layer is the entry point, receiving raw data and passing it to subsequent layers. The hidden layers, positioned between the input and output layers, capture and transform information hierarchically. Each hidden layer extracts increasingly abstract features from the input data. Finally, the output layer provides the network's prediction or classification.

The significance of layers lies in their ability to create hierarchies of abstraction. This enables neural networks to grasp intricate patterns in data. Deep neural networks with multiple hidden layers—often referred to as deep learning—excel at learning complex relationships and features from vast datasets. This depth facilitates the identification of intricate patterns and structures that might remain concealed in shallow architectures.

Layers hold the key to the network's capacity for understanding and learning. Their arrangement and size impact a model's capacity to capture both local and global features, highlighting the importance of selecting an architecture tailored to the task at hand.

Activation functions infuse neural networks with the capacity to model complex, nonlinear relationships—a hallmark of human-like learning. These functions determine the output of individual neurons based on their inputs, effectively introducing nonlinearity into the network's computations.

Activation functions range from simple, like the sigmoid and hyperbolic tangent (tanh), to modern advancements like Rectified Linear Units (ReLU) and variants. The sigmoid and tanh functions squeeze input values into a specific range, rendering them suitable for tasks requiring normalized outputs. ReLU, on the other hand, maintains the positive values while filtering out negative ones, accelerating training by mitigating the vanishing gradient problem—a phenomenon where gradients diminish as they propagate through layers.

Activation functions transform the output of neurons, enabling neural networks to capture complex relationships in data. Their nonlinearity imparts the network with the ability to model intricate patterns, making them essential for approximating the nonlinear functions present in real-world data.

The choice of activation function influences both training and performance. Selecting an appropriate function hinges on the task's requirements and the characteristics of the data. Different activation functions have distinct behaviors with respect to gradients, saturation, and computational efficiency, thereby impacting training convergence and preventing vanishing gradients.

The methodology of layers involves defining their type, arrangement, and size. Deciding on the number of hidden layers and neurons requires careful consideration, as overly complex architectures might lead to overfitting, while excessively simple architectures might lack the capacity to capture complex relationships.

The methodology of activation functions involves applying the chosen function to the weighted sum of inputs and biases within a neuron. This introduces nonlinearity into the computations, allowing the network to approximate complex functions. Activation functions should strike a balance between preserving essential information and preventing the network from becoming overly sensitive to minor variations.

Choosing the maximun number of layers and neurons is a challenge. While deep networks are adept at learning intricate patterns, they demand more data and computational resources. Striking a balance between complexity and generalization is crucial.

The selection of activation functions comes with challenges like gradient explosion and vanishing gradients. These issues can hinder training by causing unstable or slow convergence. Regularization techniques, like dropout and batch normalization, help mitigate these challenges by enhancing stability and improving training dynamics.

Layers and activation functions are the bedrock of neural networks, contributing to their transformative potential across domains. In image analysis, convolutional neural networks leverage hierarchical layers to detect intricate visual features. In natural language processing, recurrent neural networks capture sequential relationships for language understanding. In recommendation systems, feedforward networks with appropriate activation functions learn complex user preferences.

The transformative potential of these building blocks extends to diverse fields. In drug discovery, neural networks predict molecular interactions for drug design. In finance, they model market dynamics for risk assessment. In healthcare, they diagnose diseases from medical images using deep architectures.

While layers and activation functions empower neural networks, their responsible use is paramount. Ethical considerations include transparency and fairness. Models with complex architectures might be challenging to interpret, potentially hindering transparency. Ensuring that activation functions do not inadvertently introduce bias is essential for responsible deployment.

Layers and activation functions constitute the core machinery of neural networks—a symphony of interconnected computations that capture the essence of human learning and cognition. As industries traverse the frontiers of data-driven innovation, these building blocks remain guiding lights, adapting and evolving to meet the challenges of modern AI. Their legacy is etched in the hierarchical representations they unravel, the intricate patterns they unveil, and the symphony of computations that continue to shape the future of intelligence.

Convolutional Neural Networks (CNNs) for Image Data

In the realm of artificial intelligence, where algorithms strive to replicate human cognition, Convolutional Neural Networks (CNNs) stand as monumental achievements—a testament to humanity's quest to unravel the mysteries of visual intelligence. This section embarks on a journey through the intricate tapestry of CNNs, delving into their essence, methodologies, significance, and transformative role in shaping the landscape of modern image analysis.

At the heart of the digital world's quest to understand and interpret visual data lie Convolutional Neural Networks. These specialized networks are uniquely designed to process and analyze images, capturing intricate patterns, features, and hierarchies of information that define visual content. While traditional neural networks can be used for image data, CNNs are tailored to exploit the inherent structure and spatial relationships present in images.

The defining feature of CNNs is the convolutional layer— a remarkable innovation that enables the network to automatically learn and extract visual features from the data. These layers employ filters or kernels to perform convolutions over the input, capturing localized features such as edges, corners, and textures.

The significance of CNNs in image analysis is profound. They have redefined the boundaries of computer vision, enabling machines to recognize objects, classify images, and even generate new visual content. Their ability to automatically learn hierarchical features from images has led to transformative advancements in fields like medical imaging, autonomous driving, and facial recognition.

CNNs' capacity to capture both spatial and semantic information in images has fostered their use in understanding the context of visual data. They not only excel in image classification tasks but also in tasks like object detection, image segmentation, and even generating captions for images—bridging the gap between pixels and semantics.

The methodology of CNNs revolves around the interplay of convolutional and pooling layers. Convolutional layers use filters to convolve over the input, producing feature maps that capture various visual aspects. These layers are designed to automatically learn filters that can identify edges, textures, and higher-level features.

Pooling layers follow convolutional layers and serve to downsample the feature maps, reducing computational complexity while preserving essential information. Common pooling techniques include max-pooling, which extracts the maximum value from a local region, and average pooling, which computes the average value.

Architectural innovations like transfer learning have empowered the use of CNNs even with limited data. Transfer learning involves leveraging a pre-trained CNN on a large dataset and fine-tuning it on a smaller dataset particular to the task at hand. This approach capitalizes on the features learned by the CNN on the initial dataset, providing a head start for training on a different but related task.

CNNs come in various architectures, each with specific strengths. LeNet, AlexNet, VGGNet, GoogLeNet, and ResNet are some notable variants. These architectures differ in terms of depth, width, and use of convolutional layers. Deeper networks capture more complex features but require more data and computational resources. Architectural choices hinge on the trade-off between model complexity and available resources.

CNNs are not without challenges. The sheer complexity of deep architectures demands substantial computational power for training and inference. Overfitting—where models learn to memorize training data rather than generalize—is another concern. Techniques like dropout, regularization, and data augmentation address this issue. The choice of hyperparameters, including learning rates, batch sizes, and filter sizes, can greatly impact CNN performance. Fine-tuning these parameters requires iterative experimentation and tuning.

CNNs' applications span diverse domains. In healthcare, they assist in disease diagnosis from medical images. In autonomous driving, they detect pedestrians, vehicles, and traffic signs. In entertainment, they power facial recognition in unlocking devices. In agriculture, they monitor crop health and growth.

The transformative potential of CNNs extends to domains demanding visual understanding. In art, they create art-inspired images. In astronomy, they analyze celestial images for object detection. In fashion, they recommend clothing items based on visual preferences.

With great power comes great responsibility. CNNs' widespread use raises ethical considerations. Biased training data can lead to biased predictions, perpetuating inequalities. Responsible use involves diverse and representative training data, as well as continuous monitoring and assessment of model behavior.

Convolutional Neural Networks have become the cornerstone of modern computer vision and image analysis. Their ability to capture visual hierarchies, detect patterns, and understand the context of images has transformed the way machines perceive and interpret the visual world. As industries continue to unlock the potential of visual data, CNNs remain steadfast companions, adapting and evolving to meet the challenges of modern image analysis. Their legacy is etched in the intricate convolutions they perform, the patterns they unveil, and the symphony of visual understanding that continues to shape the future of intelligence.

Recurrent Neural Networks (RNNs) for Sequential Data

In the vast realm of artificial intelligence, where algorithms aspire to mimic human cognition, Recurrent Neural Networks (RNNs) stand as beacons of temporal intelligence—a testament to humanity's endeavor to comprehend and predict sequences of events. This section embarks on an exploration of RNNs, delving into their essence, methodologies, significance, and transformative role in deciphering the intricate patterns hidden within sequential data.

At the heart of the digital landscape's quest to decode the intricacies of sequential data lie Recurrent Neural Networks. These specialized networks are designed to handle data with a temporal dimension, such as time series, text, and audio. Unlike traditional feedforward neural networks that process data in isolation, RNNs possess a memory element that enables them to capture information from previous time steps and use it to influence the processing of current inputs.

The defining feature of RNNs is their recurrent connection, which allows information to flow from one time step to the next. This looping mechanism imbues RNNs with the ability to model sequences, making them exceptionally well-suited for tasks like language modeling, speech recognition, and even generating new sequences.

The significance of RNNs in sequential data analysis is profound. They have revolutionized fields like natural language processing, where understanding context and relationships between words is paramount. RNNs' temporal awareness enables them to capture patterns and dependencies that static models cannot discern. This temporal context facilitates applications like sentiment analysis, machine translation, and speech synthesis.

Furthermore, RNNs serve as building blocks for more sophisticated architectures like Long Short-Term Memory (LSTM) networks and Gated Recurrent Units (GRUs). These variants address the vanishing gradient problem—an issue that hinders the training of deep RNNs—enabling the networks to capture longer-term dependencies and patterns.

The methodology of RNNs revolves around their recurrent structure. At each time step, the network receives an input and combines it with the output of the previous time step. This iterative process enables RNNs to maintain a memory of previous inputs and their influence on the current output.

Despite their power, traditional RNNs face challenges like vanishing and exploding gradients, where gradients either become very small or very large during training. This limits their ability to capture long-range dependencies in sequences. LSTM and GRU networks alleviate these challenges by introducing gating mechanisms that regulate the flow of information through the network.

Long Short-Term Memory (or LSTM) networks and Gated Recurrent Units (or GRUs) are architectural innovations that enhance the capabilities of RNNs. LSTMs incorporate memory cells, input gates, forget gates, and output gates, allowing them to capture long-range dependencies by controlling what information is stored and retrieved at each time step.

GRUs are a simplified version of LSTMs, merging the input and forget gates into one update gate. This reduces the number of parameters and computations, making GRUs computationally more efficient while still retaining the ability to capture complex dependencies.

RNNs come with their set of challenges. The vanishing gradient problem, which affects the training of deep networks, hampers the capture of long-term dependencies. Techniques like gradient clipping and architectural innovations like LSTMs and GRUs address this issue.

The choice of network architecture and hyperparameters, like the number of hidden units and the learning rate, greatly affects performance. Balancing model complexity with available computational resources is crucial.
RNNs' applications span various domains. In natural language processing, they model text generation, language translation, and sentiment analysis. In finance,

they predict stock prices and financial trends. In healthcare, they analyze patient data for disease diagnosis and prognosis.

The transformative potential of RNNs extends to tasks demanding temporal understanding. In video analysis, they detect and track objects. In music composition, they generate melodies and harmonies. In speech recognition, they transcribe spoken language into text.

RNNs' powerful capabilities also raise ethical considerations. Bias in training data can lead to biased predictions, perpetuating inequalities. Responsible use involves diverse and representative training data and continuous monitoring to ensure fair and ethical behavior.

Recurrent Neural Networks are the bedrock of temporal intelligence within the realm of artificial intelligence. Their ability to capture sequences, remember context, and model dependencies has transformed the way machines understand and predict events over time. As industries continue to harness the potential of sequential data, RNNs remain steadfast companions, adapting and evolving to meet the challenges of modern temporal analysis. Their legacy is etched in the loops of information they traverse, the patterns they unravel, and the symphony of temporal understanding that continues to shape the future of intelligence.

CHAPTER VIII

Model Training and Evaluation

Data Splitting for Training and Testing

In the landscape of data-driven decision-making, where algorithms strive to uncover insights and predict outcomes, the art of data splitting stands as a critical cornerstone—a pathway to ensuring the reliability and generalizability of machine learning models. This section embarks on a journey through the intricate terrain of data splitting, unraveling its essence, methodologies, significance, and its transformative role in shaping the landscape of model evaluation and deployment.

Data splitting is a strategic approach to handling datasets that aims to strike a balance between model development and evaluation. The core principle involves partitioning the available data into subsets that serve distinct purposes. The two primary subsets are the training set, which is used to train the model, and the testing (or validation) set, which is used to assess the model's performance.

In essence, data splitting simulates the real-world scenario of deploying a model on unseen data. By keeping a portion of the data separate from the training process, the model's performance can be evaluated on new, unseen examples, providing a measure of its generalization ability.

The significance of data splitting lies in its role as a safeguard against overfitting—a phenomenon where a model learns to perform exceptionally good on the training data but fails to generalize to new data. Overfitting can lead to inaccurate predictions and undermine the model's utility in real-world applications.

Data splitting enables the estimation of a model's performance on unseen data, providing insights into its actual effectiveness. Without a proper evaluation dataset, the true performance of a model might remain unknown, leading to potentially misguided decisions.

The methodology of data splitting involves dividing the dataset into training and testing sets while ensuring that the two sets are mutually exclusive. The most common approach is the holdout method, where a fixed percentage of the data is randomly allocated to the testing set, and the remaining data is used for training. A variation of this is the k-fold cross-validation method, where the data is split into k subsets (folds), and the model is trained and tested k times, with each fold serving as the testing set once.

Stratified sampling is used when dealing with imbalanced classes—ensuring that the distribution of classes in the testing and training sets is representative of the overall distribution. Time-based splitting is employed in time series data to preserve the temporal order during partitioning.

The choice of splitting ratios—how much data is allocated to training versus testing—plays a pivotal role in model evaluation. While larger training sets allow models to learn more complex relationships, smaller training sets can lead to underfitting—a scenario where the model fails to capture important patterns. Balancing requires an understanding of the dataset's size, complexity, and the inherent trade-off between training and testing data.

Data splitting isn't without challenges. Random splitting might inadvertently introduce bias or result in an uneven distribution of classes between the training and testing sets. Stratified sampling and techniques like oversampling and undersampling are employed to address class imbalance.

In time series data, the temporal order must be preserved, requiring careful consideration when splitting. The choice of the number of folds in k-fold cross-validation can affect the trade-off between computational resources and model evaluation accuracy.

The applications of data splitting are manifold. In medical diagnosis, models are evaluated on a separate dataset to ensure their accuracy in identifying diseases. In finance, algorithms predict market trends based on training data while being evaluated on unseen market data. In natural language processing, models are tested on new text samples to assess their language understanding capabilities.

The transformative potential of data splitting extends to domains demanding reliable model performance. In autonomous driving, algorithms are evaluated on novel road scenarios. In fraud detection, models are assessed on unseen transaction data. In customer segmentation, algorithms are tested on new customer profiles.

Ethical considerations in data splitting revolve around ensuring that the testing set is representative of real-world scenarios and is free from biases. Biased or non-representative testing data can lead to inaccurate evaluations and biased model decisions. Responsible data splitting involves careful data curation, considering potential sources of bias and ensuring fairness in the evaluation process.

Data splitting is the compass that guides the journey from model development to deployment, ensuring that algorithms are equipped to tackle real-world challenges. Its significance lies in its ability to provide an unbiased measure of a model's effectiveness, safeguarding against overfitting and erroneous conclusions. As industries continue to leverage the power of data-driven insights, data splitting remains an indispensable practice, adapting and evolving to meet the difficulties of modern model evaluation. Its legacy is etched in the partitions it creates, the generalization it fosters, and the symphony of reliable model evaluation that continues to shape the future of intelligent decision-making.

Cross-Validation Techniques

In the realm of machine learning and data analysis, where algorithms strive to uncover patterns and insights from data, cross-validation techniques stand as a beacon of reliability—a pathway to robustly assessing the performance of models and ensuring their generalizability. This section embarks on a comprehensive exploration of cross-validation techniques, delving into their essence, methodologies, significance, and their transformative role in shaping the landscape of model evaluation and deployment.

Cross-validation techniques are a set of strategies designed to mitigate the limitations of traditional data splitting by providing more accurate estimates of a model's performance. Traditional data splitting often involves dividing the dataset into training and testing sets, with a portion reserved for evaluation. However, this approach can be problematic, as the performance estimate may vary significantly based on the specific partitioning of the data.

Cross-validation addresses this issue by systematically partitioning the data into multiple subsets, training and evaluating the model on different combinations of these subsets. The data is split into k folds or subsets, in k-fold cross-validation, the most popular type of cross-validation. Each fold serves as the testing set once as the model gets trained on k-1 folds and tested on the remaining fold. This process is repeated k times.

The significance of cross-validation lies in its ability to provide a more robust and accurate estimate of a model's performance. By repeatedly training and evaluating the model on different subsets of the data, cross-validation reduces the dependency on a specific data split and provides a more reliable assessment of how the model is likely to perform on unseen data.

Cross-validation is particularly crucial when dealing with limited datasets, as it allows for maximum utilization of available data for both training and testing. It also aids in hyperparameter tuning, as different hyperparameter values can be evaluated across multiple folds to identify the optimal configuration.

There are multiple steps in the cross-validation approach. The initial step in k-fold cross-validation is to split the data into k subsets. After training on k-1 subsets, the model is assessed on the remaining fold. Every fold serves as the testing set once during the k repetitions of this operation. The performance metrics, such as accuracy or mean squared error, are then averaged across all folds to obtain a comprehensive performance estimate.

Stratified k-fold cross-validation maintains the class distribution in each fold, ensuring a representative sample for each class. Leave-One-Out Cross-Validation (or LOOCV) is a special case of k-fold cross-validation where each fold contains only one data point, providing a more rigorous but computationally expensive assessment.

Cross-validation techniques offer several advantages. They provide a more accurate assessment of model performance, reducing the risk of overfitting or underestimating the model's generalization capabilities. Cross-validation also allows for better utilization of available data, which is particularly important in scenarios with limited samples.

However, cross-validation can be computationally intensive, as the model needs to be trained and evaluated multiple times. The choice of the number of folds (k) is crucial—it affects the trade-off between computational resources and performance estimation accuracy. Smaller values of k result in a higher variance of performance estimates, while larger values increase the computational burden.

The applications of cross-validation techniques are diverse. In medical diagnosis, models are rigorously evaluated on different subsets of patient data to ensure their reliability in identifying diseases. In finance, algorithms are assessed using various data partitions to predict market trends. In natural language processing, models are tested on different text samples to assess their language understanding capabilities.

The transformative potential of cross-validation extends to domains demanding reliable model assessment. In autonomous systems, models are evaluated using different training subsets to ensure robust performance in various scenarios. In recommendation systems, algorithms are validated using diverse user profiles to enhance personalized recommendations. In climate science, models are tested with different climate datasets to evaluate their predictive accuracy.

Ethical considerations in cross-validation include ensuring that the evaluation process is transparent and unbiased. Proper partitioning of the data, especially in cases of class imbalance, is essential to avoid biased evaluations. Responsible use involves documenting the cross-validation process, reporting the performance metrics, and being transparent about any hyperparameter tuning.

Cross-validation techniques are the bedrock of reliable model assessment within the realm of machine learning. Their ability to provide robust performance estimates, mitigate overfitting, and enhance the generalizability of models has transformed the way algorithms are evaluated and deployed. As industries continue to harness the power of data-driven insights, cross-validation remains an indispensable practice, adapting and evolving to meet the challenges of modern model evaluation. Its legacy is etched in the folds it creates, the diverse partitions it forms, and the symphony of robust model assessment that continues to shape the future of intelligent decision-making.

Hyperparameter Tuning

In the realm of machine learning, where algorithms strive to uncover patterns and insights from data, hyperparameter tuning stands as a crucial beacon—an avenue to unlocking the true potential of models and ensuring their optimal performance. This section embarks on an exploration of hyperparameter tuning, delving into its essence, methodologies, significance, and its transformative role in shaping the landscape of model optimization and deployment.

Hyperparameter tuning refers to the process of fine-tuning the parameters of a machine learning model that are not learned during training. These parameters, known as hyperparameters, govern the behavior and architecture of the model and play a pivotal role in its performance. Unlike the parameters learned through optimization algorithms like gradient descent, hyperparameters need to be set manually before training. Hyperparameters include variables like learning rate, batch size, number of hidden layers, number of neurons in each layer, regularization strength, and activation functions. Proper tuning of these hyperparameters can significantly impact a model's convergence, generalization ability, and overall performance.

The significance of hyperparameter tuning lies in its capacity to elevate the performance of machine learning models from mediocrity to excellence. A well-tuned model can drastically improve its ability to learn from data, generalize to unseen examples, and provide reliable predictions. Ignoring hyperparameter tuning or setting them arbitrarily can lead to suboptimal results, wasted computational resources, and even hinder the model's ability to learn meaningful patterns.

Hyperparameter tuning is particularly critical when dealing with complex models, large datasets, or challenging tasks. It allows models to adapt to the unique characteristics of the data and the problem domain, resulting in more accurate and effective predictions.

Hyperparameter tuning involves several methodologies, ranging from manual tuning to automated optimization techniques. Manual tuning involves iteratively adjusting hyperparameters based on domain knowledge and intuition. While this approach can yield reasonable results, it is time-consuming and might not guarantee optimal settings.

Grid Search is a systematic method to hyperparameter tuning, where a predefined set of hyperparameter values is exhaustively searched. Random Search, on the other hand, randomly samples hyperparameter values from specified ranges. Bayesian Optimization employs probabilistic models to model the objective function and select hyperparameters that maximize performance.

Hyperparameter tuning strategies vary based on the characteristics of the problem and available resources. In cases where computational resources are limited, manual tuning or small-scale grid searches might be more feasible. For complex models and ample resources, automated approaches like Bayesian Optimization or random search can be highly effective.

Challenges in hyperparameter tuning include the curse of dimensionality, where the search space becomes exponentially large as the number of hyperparameters increases. Moreover, tuning one hyperparameter might affect the performance of others, making the process intricate and requiring careful consideration.

The applications of hyperparameter tuning span diverse domains. In image analysis, optimized hyperparameters enhance the performance of convolutional neural networks in object detection tasks. In natural language processing, tuned hyperparameters improve the accuracy of language models in text classification. In finance, fine-tuned models accurately predict market trends, aiding investment decisions.

The transformative potential of hyperparameter tuning extends to tasks demanding precise and reliable predictions. In autonomous systems, tuned hyperparameters ensure robust performance in various scenarios. In healthcare, optimized hyperparameters lead to accurate disease diagnosis from medical images. In recommendation systems, tuned models provide personalized and relevant recommendations to users.

Ethical considerations in hyperparameter tuning involve ensuring transparency and reproducibility. Proper documentation of the tuning process, including the range of hyperparameter values considered, prevents the risk of introducing bias or cherry-picking results. Responsible use includes avoiding excessive tuning that might lead to overfitting on the validation data.

Hyperparameter tuning is the compass that guides machine learning models on their journey from average to exceptional performance. Its ability to shape the architecture and behavior of models, adapt them to the data's intricacies, and enhance their predictive capabilities has transformed the way algorithms are developed and deployed. As industries continue to harness the power of data-driven insights, hyperparameter tuning remains a fundamental practice, adapting and evolving to meet the difficulties of modern model optimization. Its legacy is etched in the fine adjustments it makes, the optimizations it uncovers, and the symphony of optimized models that continues to shape the future of intelligent decision-making.

Overfitting and Regularization

In the realm of machine learning, where algorithms endeavor to uncover patterns and insights from data, the delicate balance between overfitting and regularization stands as a defining challenge—a constant pursuit of extracting meaningful signals while avoiding noise. This section embarks on an exploration of overfitting and regularization, delving into their essence, methodologies, significance, and their transformative role in shaping the landscape of model performance and robustness.

Overfitting and regularization are opposing forces that play a pivotal role in the performance of machine learning models. Overfitting is a case that happens when a model learns the training data too good, capturing not only the underlying patterns but also the noise and random fluctuations present in the data. As a result, an overfitted model performs exceptionally good on the training data but fails to generalize to new, unseen examples.

Regularization, on the other hand, is a set of techniques aimed at mitigating overfitting by introducing constraints on the model's complexity. These constraints discourage the model from fitting noise and encourage it to focus on capturing the true underlying patterns in the data. Regularization techniques help strike a balance between fitting the training data well and ensuring the model's ability to generalize to new data.

The significance of overfitting and regularization lies in their profound impact on a model's predictive performance. Overfitting can lead to misleadingly high training accuracy, but the model's performance on new data is likely to be poor. Regularization techniques counteract this by guiding the model to prioritize the most relevant features and relationships, enhancing its generalization ability and making it more reliable in real-world applications.

Achieving the right balance between model complexity and regularization is crucial. A model that is too simple may not capture the underlying patterns, while a model that is too complex may fit noise. Regularization ensures that models remain interpretable, stable, and better suited for decision-making.

Regularization techniques encompass various strategies, each with its unique approach to constraining model complexity. L1 regularization (Lasso) involves adding a penalty term to the loss function based on the absolute values of the model's coefficients, promoting sparsity by forcing some coefficients to become exactly zero. L2 regularization (Ridge) adds a penalty term based on the squared values of the coefficients, encouraging small and uniform coefficients.

Elastic Net regularization combines L1 and L2 regularization, offering a balance between feature selection and coefficient shrinkage. Dropout regularization, commonly used in neural networks, involves randomly setting a fraction of neurons' outputs to zero during training, preventing the network from relying heavily on specific neurons.

Overfitting and regularization are entwined in the bias-variance trade-off—a fundamental concept in machine learning. The error introduced by approximating a real-world problem with a simplified model is known as bias. Variance, on the other hand, refers to the model's sensitivity to fluctuations in the training data.
While overfitting reduces bias by fitting the training data closely, it increases variance, leading to poor

generalization. Regularization addresses this by introducing a controlled amount of bias through constraints, which in turn reduces variance. Balancing bias and variance is essential for optimal model performance.

The applications of overfitting and regularization span diverse domains. In medical diagnosis, overfitting can lead to inaccurate disease predictions, while regularization techniques ensure reliable diagnoses. In finance, an overfitted model may lead to erroneous investment decisions, whereas regularization ensures robust financial predictions. In natural language processing, regularization techniques improve language models' generalization in text classification tasks.

The transformative potential of addressing overfitting and applying regularization techniques extends to tasks demanding precise and reliable predictions. In autonomous systems, models prevent overfitting to ensure safe navigation in various environments. In customer segmentation, models avoid fitting noise to provide meaningful insights into customer behavior. In climate science, overfitting can lead to inaccurate climate predictions, while regularization ensures better long-term forecasts.

Ethical considerations in overfitting and regularization involve ensuring the model's reliability and transparency. Overfitting can lead to biased predictions or misleading recommendations, impacting real-world decisions. Responsible use involves rigorous model validation, transparent documentation of regularization techniques, and honest reporting of model performance.

Overfitting and regularization are the scales upon which machine learning models' precision and generalization are weighed. Their dynamic interplay shapes the performance and reliability of models, guiding them to uncover meaningful insights while avoiding noise. As industries continue to harness the power of data-driven insights, the battle against overfitting and the art of regularization remain central practices, adapting and evolving to meet the challenges of modern model development. Their legacy is etched in the delicate equilibrium they establish, the noise they filter, and the symphony of balanced model performance that continues to shape the future of intelligent decision-making.

CHAPTER IX

Deploying Machine Learning Models

Model Deployment Methods

In the ever-evolving landscape of data-driven decision-making, where algorithms unearth insights from data, the bridge between model development and real-world impact lies in effective model deployment methods. This section embarks on a journey through the realm of model deployment, unraveling its essence, methodologies, significance, and its transformative role in shaping the trajectory from insights to actionable outcomes.

Model deployment is the critical phase where machine learning models transition from the laboratory to real-world applications. It involves making the model accessible and operational, allowing it to generate predictions, classifications, or recommendations in response to new data inputs. Effective model deployment ensures that the value extracted from data translates into meaningful and actionable insights.

Model deployment methods encompass a spectrum of strategies, each tailored to the specific use case and environment. These methods determine how the model interacts with users, systems, and applications, ensuring seamless integration into decision-making processes.

The significance of model deployment lies in its ability to close the loop between data-driven insights and practical impact. A well-developed model might yield valuable predictions, but its true value is realized when those predictions inform decisions, optimize processes, or drive innovation. Effective deployment transforms data-driven insights into tangible outcomes, unlocking the potential to enhance efficiency, accuracy, and informed decision-making across industries.

Model deployment also enables iterative improvement. Once in the real world, a model can collect feedback and new data, allowing for continuous learning and refinement. This adaptability is crucial in dynamic environments where data distribution or user behavior evolves over time.

Model deployment methodologies span a range of approaches, from traditional to modern techniques. In the traditional approach, models are deployed as standalone applications, integrated into existing systems, or delivered as part of software packages. These approaches often require careful engineering and integration efforts to ensure compatibility and reliability.

Modern deployment techniques leverage cloud computing platforms and containerization technologies. Cloud deployment allows models to be hosted remotely, offering scalability, flexibility, and easy access. Containers, using tools like Docker, encapsulate the model and its dependencies, ensuring consistent behavior across different environments.

Model deployment strategies vary based on factors such as the nature of the application, the target audience, and the required response time. For real-time applications, where low latency is essential, models might be deployed using microservices architecture. Batch processing applications, on the other hand, can utilize periodic batch deployments.

Ethical considerations in model deployment involve ensuring that the predictions or recommendations made by the model align with ethical guidelines and fairness principles. Biased or discriminatory predictions can have far-reaching consequences, emphasizing the need for responsible and unbiased deployment.

The applications of effective model deployment are diverse. In healthcare, deployed models aid in disease diagnosis and treatment recommendations. In e-commerce, models drive personalized recommendations to customers. In autonomous systems, deployed models enable self-driving vehicles to make real-time decisions depending on sensor data. In fraud detection, models flag suspicious transactions in real-time.

The transformative potential of model deployment extends to domains demanding immediate action and reliable decision-making. In disaster response, deployed models predict and track natural disasters, enabling timely evacuation plans. In manufacturing, models optimize production processes, reducing waste and maximizing efficiency. In energy management, deployed models optimize energy consumption, minimizing costs and environmental impact.

Ethical considerations in model deployment encompass transparency, accountability, and privacy. Models should be transparent in their decision-making process, allowing users to understand how predictions are generated. Accountability involves taking responsibility for model behavior and performance. Privacy considerations are crucial when dealing with sensitive data, requiring data anonymization and adherence to privacy regulations. Model deployment is the conduit through which data-driven insights materialize into actionable outcomes. Its role is pivotal in driving impact and transformation across industries. As industries continue to harness the power of data-driven decision-making, the art of model deployment remains a fundamental practice, adapting and evolving to meet the challenges of modern applications. Its legacy is etched in the solutions it empowers, the efficiencies it enhances, and the symphony of transformed decision-making that continues to shape the future of intelligent systems.

Considerations for Production Environments

In the realm of machine learning, where algorithms strive to transform data into actionable insights, the journey from development to production environments introduces a host of challenges and considerations. This section embarks on an exploration of the critical considerations for production environments, delving into their essence, methodologies, significance, and their transformative role in ensuring reliable, scalable, and efficient machine learning deployments.

Considerations for production environments encompass a spectrum of factors that arise when transitioning machine learning models from development to real-world applications. These factors include scalability, reliability, maintainability, performance optimization, security, and monitoring. Successful deployment in production hinges on addressing these considerations, as they ensure that models can withstand the demands of real-world usage, deliver value consistently, and align with business objectives.

The significance of production considerations lies in their role as guardians of machine learning solutions' effectiveness, efficiency, and reliability in real-world scenarios. Models that perform well in isolated development environments might falter under the pressures of real-time user demands, large-scale data inputs, and dynamic conditions. By addressing production considerations, organizations can unlock the true potential of their machine learning investments, ensuring that the insights generated are actionable, valuable, and trustworthy.

Failure to account for production considerations can result in system crashes, unreliable predictions, security breaches, and performance bottlenecks. Properly addressing these considerations enhances user satisfaction, minimizes downtime, and maximizes the return on investment in machine learning initiatives.

Addressing production considerations involves a strategic blend of methodologies and techniques. Scalability is achieved through the use of distributed systems and cloud computing platforms, allowing models to handle increased workloads. Reliability is ensured by implementing redundancy, failover mechanisms, and error handling procedures. Maintainability involves maintaining clean and well-documented code, making updates and enhancements seamless.

Performance optimization techniques include model compression, which reduces the model's size while retaining its accuracy, and hardware acceleration, which leverages specialized hardware for faster inference.

Security measures involve encryption of sensitive data, access controls, and regular vulnerability assessments. Monitoring tools and dashboards provide insights into model performance, resource utilization, and potential issues.

One of the key challenges in production environments is striking the right balance between complexity and simplicity. While complex architectures and solutions might promise advanced features, they can also introduce points of failure, maintenance challenges, and scalability issues. Simpler solutions, on the other hand, might lack certain capabilities but are often more reliable, easier to manage, and require less overhead.

The choice between complexity and simplicity depends on factors such as the nature of the application, the available resources, the required speed of deployment, and the trade-offs between performance and maintainability.

The applications of addressing production considerations are diverse. In autonomous systems, reliable deployments ensure safe navigation and decision-making in real-world environments. In finance, scalability and reliability are crucial for handling a high volume of transactions and predictions. In healthcare, models need to handle diverse patient data and deliver accurate diagnoses consistently.

The transformative potential of addressing production considerations extends to domains demanding immediate action and reliable decision-making. In disaster response, scalable and reliable systems ensure timely communication and coordination. In e-commerce, high-performance deployments provide personalized recommendations to millions of users. In energy management, optimized models control energy consumption, reducing costs and environmental impact.

Ethical considerations in production environments revolve around ensuring that the deployed models behave ethically and transparently. Models should not produce biased or discriminatory outcomes, and users should have insight into how predictions or decisions are made. Responsible deployment also involves keeping models up-to-date, applying security patches, and adhering to privacy regulations.

Addressing production considerations is the keystone of translating machine learning solutions into practical, impactful applications. The success of machine learning initiatives hinges on their ability to perform reliably, scale efficiently, and align with real-world requirements. As industries continue to leverage the power of data-driven insights, the art of addressing production considerations remains a pivotal practice, adapting and evolving to meet the demands of modern applications. Its legacy is etched in the reliability it ensures, the scalability it enables, and the symphony of seamlessly deployed machine learning solutions that continue to shape the future of intelligent systems.

Monitoring and Maintenance of Deployed Models

In the dynamic landscape of machine learning, where algorithms drive decision-making and insights, the journey doesn't conclude with model deployment—it extends into the critical phases of monitoring and maintenance. This section embarks on a comprehensive exploration of monitoring and maintenance for deployed models, unveiling their essence, methodologies, significance, and transformative role in sustaining the performance, reliability, and impact of intelligent systems.

Monitoring and maintenance are the twin pillars that ensure the continued health and effectiveness of machine learning models in production environments. Monitoring involves real-time surveillance of model performance, detecting anomalies, and ensuring that predictions align with expectations. Maintenance, on the other hand, encompasses a set of strategies to address issues, update models, and refine them based on evolving data and user needs.

The partnership between monitoring and maintenance guarantees that deployed models remain aligned with real-world dynamics, provide accurate predictions, and respond effectively to changes in data distribution or user behavior.

The significance of monitoring and maintenance lies in their capacity to bridge the gap between initial deployment and sustained value. Machine learning models are frequently deployed in dynamic environments where data distribution shifts, user preferences evolve, and external factors change. Monitoring ensures that models continue to operate effectively in such conditions, adapting to new challenges and retaining their predictive power.

Maintenance safeguards models from degradation, drift, or obsolescence. Without proper maintenance, models can fall victim to concept drift—when the underlying patterns in the data change over time—or become outdated as user expectations evolve. Monitoring and maintenance serve as the guardians of model longevity, ensuring they remain relevant, reliable, and valuable.

The methodologies for monitoring and maintenance are multi-faceted, combining technical and strategic approaches. Monitoring involves real-time tracking of performance metrics, anomaly detection through statistical methods, and alerts triggered by deviations from expected behavior. Techniques such as drift detection monitor changes in data distribution, while fairness monitoring ensures predictions remain unbiased and ethically sound.

Maintenance strategies encompass model retraining, which involves updating the model with novel data to account for changes in the environment. Incremental learning techniques allow models to learn from new data without discarding existing knowledge. Version control systems track changes made to models, ensuring transparency and reproducibility.

One of the key challenges in monitoring and maintenance is striking the right balance between automation and human intervention. Automated monitoring systems can detect anomalies and trigger alerts, but human expertise is essential to interpret anomalies, diagnose issues, and make informed decisions about model updates or interventions.

Human intervention ensures that models respond effectively to nuanced changes that might not be captured by automated systems. It also prevents overfitting to anomalies and ensures that models remain aligned with the overall goals of the organization.

The applications of monitoring and maintenance span diverse domains. In healthcare, monitoring ensures that disease prediction models adapt to changing patient populations and medical trends. In fraud detection, models need to detect emerging fraud patterns to remain effective. In recommendation systems, monitoring captures shifts in user preferences to provide relevant recommendations.

The transformative potential of monitoring and maintenance extends to domains demanding continuous performance and adaptability. In autonomous vehicles, monitoring detects sensor malfunctions and updates models to handle new road conditions. In finance, maintenance ensures that trading algorithms respond to real-time market changes effectively. In manufacturing, monitoring optimizes production processes to minimize defects.

Ethical considerations in monitoring and maintenance involve ensuring that models remain unbiased, fair, and transparent. Models should not amplify existing biases or discriminate against certain groups. Responsible maintenance involves conducting regular audits of model behavior, addressing bias or fairness issues, and adhering to privacy regulations when updating or retraining models.

Monitoring and maintenance form the backbone of intelligent systems, ensuring that the value derived from machine learning models endures over time. Their role in preserving accuracy, relevance, and reliability in dynamic environments is indispensable. As industries continue to harness the power of data-driven insights, the art of monitoring and maintenance remains a fundamental practice, adapting and evolving to meet the demands of modern applications. Their legacy is etched in the sustained impact they enable, the reliability they ensure, and the symphony of ever-evolving intelligent systems that continue to shape the future of decision-making and innovation.

CHAPTER X

Ethics and Bias in Data Science

Understanding Bias and Fairness

In the world of data science and algorithmic decision-making, the concepts of bias and fairness have emerged as critical touchpoints, commanding attention as society navigates the digital age. This section embarks on an exploration of bias and fairness in data science, delving into their intricacies, methodologies, significance, and their transformative role in shaping the ethics and accountability of algorithmic systems.

Bias in data science refers to the presence of systematic and unfair inaccuracies in data or algorithms that lead to erroneous outcomes or perpetuate discriminatory patterns. Bias can emerge at various stages of the data science pipeline, from data collection and preprocessing to model training and deployment. Types of bias include selection bias, where certain groups are underrepresented in the data, and algorithmic bias, where models learn and propagate existing biases in the data.

Bias can be unintentional, arising from the data's inherent characteristics or the algorithm's design. It can also be a result of societal biases encoded in historical data. Addressing bias is crucial to ensure that the decisions made by algorithms are fair, ethical, and unbiased.

Fairness in data science relates to the equitable treatment of individuals or groups, ensuring that algorithmic decisions do not discriminate against or disadvantage specific segments of the population. Fairness encompasses different dimensions, including demographic parity (equal outcomes for different groups), individual fairness (similar individuals receiving similar treatment), and disparate impact (avoiding unjustified disparities).

Achieving fairness involves defining fairness criteria, evaluating algorithmic fairness, and mitigating unfairness through algorithmic adjustments. However, defining fairness is complex, as different notions of fairness may conflict with one another. Balancing fairness considerations with other objectives, such as accuracy and utility, presents a challenge.

The significance of bias and fairness lies in their capacity to influence individual lives, exacerbate societal inequalities, and erode trust in algorithmic systems. Biased decisions can lead to discriminatory outcomes in areas such as criminal justice, hiring, lending, and healthcare. Such outcomes can perpetuate systemic injustices and amplify existing biases, undermining the potential of data-driven decision-making to drive positive change.

Addressing bias and ensuring fairness is not only a moral imperative but also crucial for the long-term viability of algorithmic systems. As algorithms become more integrated into daily life, their impact on society's well-being grows. Ensuring fairness is essential for preserving public trust, preventing harm, and fostering inclusive and equitable environments.

Addressing bias and ensuring fairness involves a combination of technical and ethical methodologies. Preprocessing techniques, such as reweighting or re-sampling, can balance underrepresented groups in the data. Algorithmic techniques, like adversarial training, aim to make models robust to biases. Post-processing methods, including re-ranking or re-ranking, modify model outputs to align with fairness objectives.

Ethical methodologies involve considering the societal implications of algorithms, involving stakeholders in the decision-making process, and designing mechanisms for accountability and transparency. Fairness-aware machine learning, where fairness criteria are explicitly integrated into the learning process, is a growing research area that seeks to achieve fairness while maintaining model performance.

Addressing bias and ensuring fairness is not without challenges. Defining fairness is complex and context-dependent, making it difficult to develop universal solutions. Balancing fairness with other objectives, like model accuracy, introduces trade-offs that require careful consideration. Additionally, fairness interventions can sometimes lead to unintended consequences, such as reduced predictive accuracy for certain groups.

The collection of unbiased and representative data is a foundational step in addressing bias. Ensuring diverse representation and reducing underrepresented groups' data scarcity can mitigate biased outcomes. Transparency in algorithmic decision-making is also crucial for accountability and allowing affected individuals to understand and challenge algorithmic decisions.

The applications of addressing bias and ensuring fairness are vast. In criminal justice, fairness interventions aim to reduce disparities in sentencing and pretrial release decisions. In hiring, algorithms aim to ensure equal opportunities for job applicants from diverse backgrounds. In lending, fairness considerations prevent discriminatory lending practices.

The transformative potential of addressing bias and ensuring fairness extends to domains demanding accountable and equitable decision-making. In healthcare, bias mitigation ensures that medical diagnoses and treatment recommendations are unbiased and accurate. In education, fairness interventions aim to reduce disparities in resource allocation and student evaluations. In recommendation systems, ensuring diverse and representative recommendations promotes equitable content distribution.

Ethical considerations in addressing bias and ensuring fairness involve maintaining transparency about the methods used to address bias, being transparent about the potential trade-offs between fairness and other objectives, and involving affected communities in decision-making. Responsible use involves continuous monitoring of algorithmic systems for bias, regular audits, and updates to adapt to changing societal norms and values.

Bias and fairness constitute a pivotal crossroads in the journey of data science and algorithmic decision-making. Their impact on individual lives, societal dynamics, and the integrity of intelligent systems cannot be overstated. As industries continue to leverage data-driven insights, the pursuit of unbiased, fair, and ethical algorithmic systems remains a central practice, adapting and evolving to meet the challenges of modern applications. Their legacy is etched in the equitable opportunities they create, the ethical decisions they enable, and the symphony of accountable and just algorithmic systems that continue to shape the future of decision-making and innovation.

Ethical Considerations in Data Collection and Usage

In the realm of data science, where algorithms extract insights from vast troves of information, ethical considerations surrounding data collection and usage have emerged as a critical linchpin. This section embarks on an exploration of the ethical dimensions in data collection and usage, delving into their complexities, methodologies, significance, and their transformative role in safeguarding individual rights, privacy, and the responsible utilization of data-driven insights.

Ethical considerations in data collection and usage encompass a spectrum of factors that arise when acquiring, storing, and employing data for analytical purposes. These considerations navigate the tension between the desire for extracting valuable insights and the need to respect individual privacy, consent, and societal norms. Balancing utility and the protection of individual rights lies at the heart of ethical data practices.

Data collection involves various stages, including identifying the purpose of data collection, obtaining informed consent, ensuring data anonymity, and adhering to data protection regulations. Ethical data usage extends to ensuring that the insights drawn from data do not perpetuate discrimination, bias, or harm to individuals or communities.

The significance of ethical data collection and usage is underscored by their potential to impact individuals, organizations, and societies at large. Unethical data practices, such as unauthorized data collection or the misuse of personal information, can lead to privacy breaches, trust erosion, and legal repercussions. Furthermore, decisions made based on biased or discriminatory insights can exacerbate societal inequalities and undermine the potential of data-driven decision-making to drive positive change.

Ethical data practices are fundamental to ensuring trust between data collectors, users, and the broader public. By adhering to ethical guidelines, organizations can demonstrate their commitment to responsible data management, cultivate trust, and pave the way for ethical innovations that benefit society as a whole.

Ethical data collection and usage involve a multi-faceted approach, encompassing legal frameworks, technical safeguards, and cultural considerations. Legal frameworks, like General Data Protection Regulation in Europe, stipulate guidelines for obtaining consent, data protection, and user rights. Technical measures include data anonymization, encryption, and data access controls to guarantee that sensitive information is protected.

Cultural considerations involve understanding the norms, values, and expectations of the communities from which data is collected. Data collectors must recognize that the mere fact that data can be collected does not necessarily mean it should be collected. Ensuring that data is collected for legitimate and socially responsible purposes is paramount.

One of the key challenges in ethical data collection and usage is striking the right balance between privacy and utility. Stricter data privacy measures, such as stringent consent requirements and data anonymization, can enhance privacy but may limit the utility of data for analysis. On the other hand, lax privacy measures might enable more extensive data analysis but can compromise individuals' rights and privacy.

Balancing privacy and utility requires organizations to consider the specific context of data collection and usage, the possible risks to individuals, and the potential advantages to society. Organizations must also be transparent about their data practices, clearly communicating to individuals how their data will be collected, used, and protected.

The applications of ethical data collection and usage are broad-reaching. In healthcare, ethical data practices ensure that patient information is protected while enabling medical research and diagnosis. In finance, ethical data usage prevents discriminatory lending practices while facilitating risk assessment. In social sciences, ethical data collection safeguards participants' privacy while advancing our understanding of human behavior.

The transformative potential of ethical data collection and usage extends to domains demanding responsible and informed decision-making. In education, ethical data practices ensure that student data is protected while improving learning outcomes through data-driven insights. In urban planning, ethical data collection informs city development while preserving residents' privacy. In marketing, ethical data practices prevent intrusive targeting while enhancing customer engagement.

Ethical considerations in data collection and usage involve transparency, accountability, and the principle of informed consent. Data collectors should communicate how data will be used, who will have access to it, and the steps taken to protect it. Individuals should have the agency to grant or deny consent based on clear information.

Responsible use of data involves limiting data collection to what is necessary for the intended purpose, ensuring data security, and considering the potential impact on individuals and communities. Organizations should also establish mechanisms for addressing ethical concerns, such as having a designated data ethics officer or committee.

Ethical data collection and usage stand as the moral compass guiding the data-driven landscape towards responsible, equitable, and socially beneficial outcomes. Their role in safeguarding individual rights, ensuring privacy, and promoting responsible innovation is undeniable. As industries continue to harness the power of data-driven insights, the practice of ethical data collection and usage remains a foundational principle, adapting and evolving to meet the demands of modern applications. Their legacy is etched in the respect for privacy they promote, the responsible decisions they facilitate, and the symphony of ethical data practices that continue to shape the future of decision-making and progress.

Mitigating Bias in Machine Learning Models

In the realm of machine learning, where algorithms shape decisions across various domains, the specter of bias has emerged as a formidable challenge, demanding attention and solutions. This section embarks on a comprehensive exploration of mitigating bias in machine learning models, unraveling its complexities, methodologies, significance, and its transformative role in shaping fair, accountable, and just algorithmic systems.

Bias in machine learning is the systematic and unfair inaccuracies in predictions or decisions made by algorithms, leading to unjust and discriminatory outcomes. Bias can stem from historical data, societal prejudices, or the design of algorithms. It can manifest as either disparate treatment, where different groups are treated unequally, or disparate impact, where seemingly neutral decisions disproportionately affect certain groups.

Bias in machine learning models poses ethical, legal, and social challenges. Biased models perpetuate systemic inequalities, reinforce discriminatory patterns, and undermine the potential of algorithms to drive positive societal change. Addressing bias is imperative to ensure that algorithmic decisions uphold fairness, justice, and respect for human rights.

The significance of mitigating bias in machine learning models lies in the transformation of algorithmic decision-making from perpetuating discrimination to fostering equitable opportunities. Unmitigated bias can result in biased hiring decisions, discriminatory loan approvals, and unfair criminal sentencing, amplifying societal inequalities and eroding public trust in algorithmic systems.

Mitigating bias is a fundamental step towards building algorithms that uphold the principles of fairness, transparency, and accountability. By creating models that provide equitable outcomes, organizations can ensure that algorithms positively contribute to society, amplify inclusivity, and champion social progress.

Mitigating bias in machine learning models requires a multifaceted approach, encompassing data preprocessing, algorithmic adjustments, and ongoing evaluation. Data preprocessing techniques involve data re-sampling to balance class distribution, re-weighting to reduce bias, and data augmentation to increase underrepresented groups' visibility. Bias-aware algorithms incorporate fairness constraints into the learning process, aiming to achieve equitable outcomes.

Algorithmic adjustments, such as re-ranking or re-scoring, modify model predictions to align with fairness objectives. Post-processing techniques mitigate bias by correcting predictions to ensure equal error rates or calibration across different groups. Additionally, adversarial training involves training models to be robust against attempts to infer sensitive information from their outputs.

Mitigating bias in machine learning models is a complex endeavor riddled with challenges. Defining fairness is nuanced and context-dependent, making it difficult to devise universally applicable solutions. Balancing fairness considerations with other objectives, like model accuracy and utility, introduces trade-offs that require careful consideration. Additionally, interventions aimed at mitigating bias might lead to unintended consequences, such as reduced predictive performance for certain groups.

Striking the right balance between bias mitigation and model accuracy demands ongoing evaluation, experimentation, and collaboration across multidisciplinary teams. Responsible bias mitigation also involves understanding the potential societal implications of model decisions and taking into account diverse stakeholder perspectives.

The applications of mitigating bias in machine learning models are far-reaching. In criminal justice, bias mitigation aims to reduce disparities in risk assessment and sentencing decisions. In healthcare, fair models ensure that medical diagnoses and treatment recommendations are unbiased and accurate. In hiring, bias mitigation prevents discriminatory practices in candidate selection.

The transformative potential of bias mitigation extends to domains demanding accountable and transparent decision-making. In education, fair models reduce bias in student evaluations and resource allocation. In finance, bias mitigation prevents discriminatory lending practices. In recommendation systems, ensuring diverse and representative recommendations promotes equitable content distribution.

Ethical considerations in mitigating bias involve transparency about the methods used to address bias, considering the potential trade-offs between fairness and other objectives, and involving affected communities in decision-making. Responsible mitigation involves continuous monitoring of models for bias, regular audits to detect and rectify biased behavior, and updating models to adapt to changing societal norms.

Mitigating bias in machine learning models is a transformative endeavor that reshapes algorithmic systems from perpetuating discrimination to championing equity. Its significance transcends technical intricacies, encompassing ethical imperatives, societal progress, and responsible innovation. As industries continue to harness the power of data-driven insights, the practice of mitigating bias remains a central principle, adapting and evolving to meet the challenges of modern applications. Its legacy is etched in the equitable opportunities it fosters, the just decisions it enables, and the symphony of fair algorithmic systems that continue to shape the future of decision-making and progress.

CHAPTER XI

Real-World Case Studies

Case Study 1: Predictive Maintenance in Manufacturing

In the realm of modern manufacturing, where efficiency, uptime, and cost-effectiveness are paramount, the convergence of data science and industrial operations has given rise to a groundbreaking application: predictive maintenance. This case study delves into the intricacies, methodologies, significance, and transformative impact of predictive maintenance in manufacturing, unveiling how data-driven insights are revolutionizing the way industries approach equipment maintenance and ushering in a new era of productivity and sustainability.

Predictive maintenance is a data-driven approach that leverages machine learning algorithms to forecast when industrial machinery and equipment are likely to fail. Rather than adhering to traditional time-based maintenance schedules, which may result in unnecessary downtime or untimely repairs, predictive maintenance harnesses real-time sensor data, historical performance, and advanced analytics to predict the optimal time for maintenance interventions.

By analyzing data patterns, such as vibrations, temperature variations, and fluid levels, predictive maintenance algorithms identify anomalies and deviations that indicate impending equipment failures.

This proactive approach empowers manufacturers to address maintenance needs precisely when they are required, optimizing resource allocation, minimizing downtime, and ultimately driving efficiency gains.

Predictive maintenance involves several key methodologies that collectively form a comprehensive framework for proactive equipment management. Data collection is the foundational step, where sensors and IoT devices capture real-time operational data. Data preprocessing involves cleaning, transforming, and normalizing the data to ensure its accuracy and reliability. Feature extraction identifies relevant patterns and metrics from the raw data, which serve as inputs to predictive models.

Machine learning models, such as regression, classification, or time series analysis, are then trained on historical data to predict future failures. The models learn to discern normal patterns from anomalies, allowing them to anticipate equipment malfunctions. Continuous monitoring of real-time data feeds these models, enabling them to adapt to changing conditions and refine their predictions over time.

The significance of predictive maintenance in manufacturing lies in its potential to revolutionize industrial operations, streamline maintenance practices, and optimize resource allocation. By accurately predicting equipment failures, manufacturers can shift from reactive maintenance, which addresses issues only after they occur, to a proactive and preventative approach that mitigates disruptions before they happen.

The impacts are far-reaching. Downtime caused by unexpected breakdowns is reduced, leading to increased operational efficiency and higher productivity.

Maintenance costs are optimized as resources are allocated precisely when needed, avoiding unnecessary interventions. Energy consumption is optimized as equipment operates at peak efficiency, reducing waste. Moreover, predictive maintenance extends equipment lifetimes, enhancing sustainability by reducing waste and the need for premature replacements.

The applications of predictive maintenance in manufacturing span diverse industries. In aviation, predictive maintenance ensures aircraft reliability by preemptively identifying components requiring maintenance. In energy, it minimizes downtime in power plants by foreseeing issues and optimizing maintenance schedules. In automotive manufacturing, it enhances assembly line efficiency by preventing equipment breakdowns.

The transformative potential of predictive maintenance extends beyond operational efficiency. It shifts the manufacturing paradigm from a reactive and costly maintenance approach to a proactive, data-driven, and cost-effective strategy. Industries can harness predictive maintenance to elevate their competitiveness, deliver superior product quality, and contribute to sustainable practices.

Despite its transformative potential, predictive maintenance in manufacturing presents challenges. Data quality and availability are pivotal, requiring consistent and accurate data feeds to ensure accurate predictions. Selecting the right features and models demands domain expertise and thorough analysis of data patterns. Handling edge cases and rare events, as well as addressing issues of data privacy and security, are paramount.

Moreover, predictive maintenance models must be periodically retrained to adapt to changing equipment conditions and data distributions. Balancing the costs of implementation with the expected benefits requires careful cost-benefit analysis. Additionally, stakeholder buy-in and training are crucial to ensure seamless integration of predictive maintenance practices into existing workflows.

Ethical considerations in predictive maintenance encompass responsible data handling, ensuring privacy, and preventing discriminatory practices. Data collected from equipment sensors must be anonymized and securely stored to prevent unauthorized access. Additionally, the insights derived from predictive maintenance should not be used to justify labor exploitation or the replacement of human workers without appropriate considerations.

Responsible implementation also involves transparency in communication, informing employees and stakeholders about the deployment of predictive maintenance practices. Ensuring that the benefits of predictive maintenance are shared across the organization and lead to improved working conditions fosters positive engagement and ethical practices.

Predictive maintenance in manufacturing is a testament to the transformative power of data-driven insights. By transcending traditional maintenance approaches and adopting a proactive stance, industries are unlocking operational efficiencies, minimizing disruptions, and fostering sustainability. As manufacturing continues to evolve in the digital age, the practice of predictive maintenance stands as a beacon of innovation, shaping the landscape of efficiency, competitiveness, and responsible industrial practices. Its legacy is etched in the optimized machinery it upholds, the streamlined operations it enables, and the symphony of efficient manufacturing processes that continue to shape the future of industry.

Case Study 2: Customer Segmentation in E-commerce

In the bustling realm of e-commerce, where diverse consumer preferences and purchasing behaviors intersect, the integration of data science and customer segmentation has emerged as a transformative force. This case study delves into the intricacies, methodologies, significance, and transformative impact of customer segmentation in e-commerce, unveiling how data-driven insights are revolutionizing the way businesses approach consumer engagement, personalization, and market targeting.

Customer segmentation is a data-driven strategy that divides a heterogeneous customer base into distinct segments based on shared characteristics, behaviors, and preferences. In the context of e-commerce, segmentation involves grouping customers according to factors such as purchase history, browsing behavior, demographic information, and interactions with the platform. The aim is to uncover nuanced insights that allow businesses to tailor their marketing strategies, personalize experiences, and optimize customer interactions.

By segmenting customers, e-commerce platforms can deliver targeted marketing campaigns, optimize product recommendations, and tailor communication to resonate with specific consumer groups. This personalized approach enhances customer satisfaction, increases engagement, and fosters brand loyalty in an increasingly competitive digital marketplace.

Customer segmentation in e-commerce employs a range of methodologies to analyze data and unearth meaningful segments. Data collection involves gathering customer interactions, transaction history, browsing behavior, and demographic information. Data preprocessing is performed to clean, transform, and standardize the data for analysis. Feature extraction identifies relevant attributes that distinguish customer behaviors, such as purchase frequency, average order value, or product preferences.

Clustering algorithms, like K-means or hierarchical clustering, group customers based on similarity metrics derived from the extracted features. These algorithms partition customers into segments, each characterized by distinct behaviors or characteristics. Post-segmentation analysis evaluates segment characteristics, validates segment assignments, and guides marketing strategies to cater to each segment's unique needs.

The significance of customer segmentation in e-commerce lies in its capacity to revolutionize customer engagement, marketing effectiveness, and business growth. Segmentation enables businesses to move beyond generic, one-size-fits-all approaches to marketing and communication. By understanding customer preferences, buying patterns, and behaviors, e-commerce platforms can tailor product recommendations, promotions, and communication strategies to each segment, thereby enhancing the likelihood of conversions.

Segmentation also facilitates the optimization of marketing expenditures by directing resources toward segments with higher potential returns. Businesses can allocate marketing budgets more effectively, target niche markets, and focus on customers who are more likely to respond positively to specific marketing initiatives. The result is not only increased revenue but also improved customer satisfaction and loyalty.

The applications of customer segmentation in e-commerce span a multitude of avenues. In fashion e-commerce, segmentation allows retailers to offer personalized clothing recommendations based on individual style preferences. In online grocery delivery, segmentation informs targeted promotions and product bundles to cater to diverse dietary preferences. In technology retail, segmentation tailors product recommendations based on users' prior purchase history.

The transformative potential of customer segmentation extends beyond marketing efficiency. It shapes the customer journey, from discovery to purchase, and enhances the overall shopping experience. E-commerce platforms can foster customer loyalty by creating personalized journeys, curating product assortments, and ensuring that each touchpoint resonates with specific customer segments.

Despite its transformative potential, customer segmentation in e-commerce presents challenges. Data quality and privacy are paramount, necessitating transparent data collection practices and adherence to data protection regulations. Selecting the right features for segmentation requires domain expertise and an in-depth understanding of the factors driving customer behavior. Balancing the need for granularity with the risk of over-segmentation demands careful consideration.

Additionally, segment validation and robustness are crucial. Segments must be meaningful, actionable, and stable over time. Regular monitoring and evaluation of segment performance ensure that marketing strategies remain aligned with customer behaviors and preferences.

Ethical considerations in customer segmentation involve respecting user privacy, securing sensitive data, and preventing discriminatory practices. Customer data should be anonymized and aggregated to protect individual identities. Moreover, the insights derived from segmentation should not be used to discriminate against specific customer groups or exploit vulnerable individuals.

Responsible implementation also requires transparent communication with customers about how their data is used for segmentation purposes. Platforms should offer customers the option to opt out of data collection and segmentation if they choose. Implementing segmentation with a focus on fostering positive user experiences and delivering genuine value demonstrates ethical conduct and builds trust with customers.

Customer segmentation in e-commerce is a beacon of innovation that redefines customer engagement, personalization, and marketing effectiveness. Its significance extends beyond data analytics, encompassing enhanced customer experiences, business growth, and brand loyalty. As e-commerce continues to evolve in the digital era, the practice of customer segmentation stands as a testament to the potential of data-driven insights, shaping the landscape of personalized marketing, targeted engagement, and sustainable growth. Its legacy is etched in the tailored shopping experiences it fosters, the optimized marketing strategies it enables, and the symphony of customer-centric e-commerce platforms that continue to shape the future of online retail.

Case Study 3: Medical Diagnosis using Deep Learning

In the realm of modern healthcare, where accuracy, early detection, and personalized treatment are paramount, the integration of deep learning and medical diagnosis has ushered in a transformative era. This case study delves into the intricacies, methodologies, significance, and transformative impact of medical diagnosis using deep learning, unveiling how data-driven insights are revolutionizing the way medical professionals approach disease detection, diagnosis, and patient care.

Medical diagnosis using deep learning involves harnessing the power of artificial neural networks to analyze medical data, such as images, clinical records, and patient histories. Deep learning models, mainly convolutional neural networks (or CNNs) and recurrent neural networks (RNNs), are trained on large datasets to identify patterns, anomalies, and biomarkers indicative of various medical conditions. The goal is to achieve more accurate, efficient, and early diagnoses that enable timely intervention and improved patient outcomes.

By leveraging deep learning, medical professionals can enhance diagnostic accuracy, minimize human error, and unlock insights from complex medical data. Deep learning models are capable of identifying subtle features that might escape the human eye, thereby enabling early detection and reducing the risk of missed diagnoses.

Medical diagnosis using deep learning encompasses a range of methodologies tailored to different types of medical data. For image-based diagnosis, CNNs are widely employed to extract intricate patterns from medical images, such as X-rays, MRIs, and histopathological slides. These models are trained on annotated medical images to recognize features associated with specific conditions, enabling accurate disease classification.

In text-based medical diagnosis, RNNs and transformer models analyze clinical notes, electronic health records, and medical literature to extract relevant information for diagnosis. These models capture temporal dependencies and contextual cues, facilitating accurate identification of diseases, risk factors, and treatment options.

The significance of medical diagnosis using deep learning transcends traditional diagnostic approaches, offering an array of benefits that encompass accuracy, efficiency, and personalization. Deep learning models exhibit exceptional accuracy in disease detection, surpassing human performance in certain cases. This precision enhances diagnostic confidence, facilitates early intervention, and contributes to better patient outcomes.

Efficiency gains are another hallmark of medical diagnosis using deep learning. Automated analysis of medical data reduces the burden on healthcare professionals, allowing them to allocate more time to patient care and treatment planning. Moreover, personalized diagnosis based on patients' unique biomarkers and genetic profiles enables tailored treatment strategies that optimize efficacy and minimize adverse effects.

The applications of medical diagnosis using deep learning span a multitude of medical specialties. In radiology, deep learning models assist in detecting abnormalities in medical images, from identifying tumors to pinpointing fractures. In pathology, these models analyze cellular patterns in histopathological slides to diagnose cancers and other diseases. In genomics, deep learning deciphers genetic information to predict disease susceptibility and tailor precision treatments.

The transformative potential of medical diagnosis using deep learning extends beyond diagnostic accuracy. It redefines the healthcare landscape by enabling early disease detection, reducing diagnostic timeframes, and fostering personalized treatment plans. Moreover, it paves the way for telemedicine, allowing remote patients to receive accurate diagnoses and expert medical opinions, transcending geographical barriers.

Despite its transformative potential, medical diagnosis using deep learning presents challenges. Data quality and quantity are crucial for training accurate models. Access to annotated medical datasets, which are often limited due to privacy concerns and data complexity, can hinder model performance. Moreover, models trained on biased data might propagate existing disparities in healthcare, leading to discriminatory outcomes.

Interpreting deep learning models' decisions, often referred to as the "black box" problem, is another challenge. Understanding why a model arrives at a particular diagnosis is crucial for clinical validation and decision-making. Model explainability techniques, like feature visualization and attention mechanisms, aim to address this challenge by shedding light on the factors driving model decisions.

Ethical considerations in medical diagnosis using deep learning encompass patient privacy, transparency, and responsible model deployment. Medical data should be anonymized and protected to prevent unauthorized access or breaches. Moreover, patient consent for data usage and model deployment is paramount, ensuring that individuals are informed about how their data contributes to medical research.

Responsible implementation also involves transparency in communication with patients and healthcare professionals. Clear explanations of how deep learning models function, their limitations, and the potential risks and benefits are essential for building trust and obtaining informed consent.

Medical diagnosis using deep learning epitomizes the transformative power of data-driven healthcare. By transcending traditional diagnostic approaches and embracing the potential of artificial intelligence, medical professionals are unlocking accuracy, efficiency, and personalization in disease detection and patient care. As healthcare evolves in the digital era, the practice of medical diagnosis using deep learning stands as a testament to innovation, shaping the landscape of precision medicine, early intervention, and personalized healthcare. Its legacy is etched in the timely diagnoses it enables, the optimized treatment strategies it fosters, and the symphony of accurate medical decisions that continue to transform the healthcare delivery and patient well-being future.

CHAPTER XII

The Future of Data Science and Machine Learning

Emerging Trends in the Field

The field of data science and machine learning is characterized by constant evolution and innovation, driven by advancements in technology, changing industry demands, and a growing understanding of the potential of data-driven insights. This section delves into the emerging trends that are reshaping the landscape of data science and machine learning, exploring their significance, methodologies, transformative potential, and their role in shaping the future of decision-making, innovation, and societal progress.

As data privacy concerns continue to gain prominence, federated learning has emerged as a revolutionary trend. Federated learning allows models to be trained across distributed devices while keeping data localized. This approach preserves data privacy, as sensitive information remains on users' devices, and only model updates are shared. By enabling machine learning models to learn from decentralized data sources, federated learning addresses privacy concerns and fosters collaboration among organizations without compromising individual privacy.

The "black box" nature of intricate machine learning models has been a challenge for their widespread adoption, especially in critical applications like healthcare and finance. Explainable AI (XAI) is a trend that focuses on developing models that can provide interpretable explanations for their decisions. Techniques like feature visualization, attention mechanisms, and model-agnostic explanations aim to enhance transparency, enable model validation, and build trust among users and stakeholders.

With the growth of edge computing and the Internet of Things (IoT), the integration of AI at the edge has become a prominent trend. Edge AI involves deploying machine learning models directly on edge devices, reducing latency, conserving bandwidth, and enabling real-time decision-making. This trend empowers devices like smartphones, sensors, and smart appliances to process data locally, improving efficiency and responsiveness while minimizing the need for constant data transmission to centralized servers.

The democratization of machine learning is propelled by the trend of Automated Machine Learning (AutoML). AutoML tools and platforms aim to simplify the machine learning pipeline, automating tasks such as feature selection, hyperparameter tuning, and model evaluation. This trend empowers non-experts to leverage the power of machine learning, enabling businesses to rapidly develop and deploy models without the need for extensive expertise in data science.

Reinforcement learning, a paradigm where agents learn to make decisions by interacting with an environment, has witnessed rapid advancements. While initially prominent in gaming and simulation, reinforcement learning is now making inroads into real-world applications. From optimizing supply chain management to enhancing energy efficiency in buildings, reinforcement learning is being harnessed to solve complex problems where traditional algorithms may fall short.

With the increasing influence of AI in decision-making, the ethical implications of algorithmic bias and fairness have come to the forefront. The trend of integrating AI ethics and fairness considerations involves developing methodologies to identify and mitigate biases in machine learning models. These efforts aim to ensure equitable outcomes across diverse demographic groups, promote social responsibility, and prevent discriminatory practices.

The nascent field of quantum machine learning combines the power of quantum computing with the machine learning algorithms. Quantum computers have the ability to solve intricate optimization problems and perform calculations exponentially faster than classical computers. Quantum machine learning is poised to revolutionize industries such as cryptography, drug discovery, and financial modeling by tackling computational challenges that were previously insurmountable.

Emerging trends in data science and in machine learning are moving towards leveraging multiple sources of data, known as multi-modal learning. This approach integrates information from various modalities, such as text, images, and audio, to enhance model performance and enrich insights. Similarly, transfer learning, where pre-trained models are fine-tuned for specific tasks, is gaining traction. These trends allow models to leverage knowledge learned from one domain to improve performance in another, accelerating model training and reducing data requirements.

Synthetic data generation and data augmentation are trends addressing the challenge of data scarcity.

Synthetic data is artificially created to mimic real-world data, enabling the training of models in scenarios where obtaining sufficient real data is challenging. Data augmentation involves applying transformations to existing data, effectively increasing the diversity of training examples. These trends enhance model robustness, improve generalization, and address bias in training datasets.

The field of data science and machine learning is in a state of perpetual evolution, driven by the relentless pursuit of insights and innovation. The trends discussed here exemplify the dynamism of the field, from privacy-preserving techniques that safeguard individual data to quantum machine learning that taps into the potential of quantum computing. As industries continue to harness the power of data-driven insights, the emerging trends in data science and machine learning stand as beacons of progress, guiding the path toward responsible innovation, equitable decision-making, and transformative societal change. Their legacy is etched in the algorithms that enable us to see beyond the present, the solutions that address the challenges of tomorrow, and the symphony of advancements that continue to shape the future of human endeavors.

AI and Machine Learning in Various Industries

The Artificial Intelligence (AI) and Machine Learning (ML) integration is ushering in a new era of innovation, efficiency, and transformation across diverse industries. This section delves into how AI and ML are revolutionizing sectors ranging from healthcare to finance, manufacturing to agriculture, exploring their methodologies, applications, transformative potential, and the role they play in shaping the future of industries, economies, and societies.

In healthcare, AI and ML are shaping the landscape of diagnosis, treatment, and patient care. AI-powered diagnostic tools analyze medical images, such as X-rays and MRIs, with remarkable accuracy. Deep learning models detect anomalies and early signs of diseases, enhancing the speed and accuracy of diagnosis. Personalized treatment plans are also being developed through AI-driven analysis of genetic data, enabling tailored therapies based on patients' unique genetic profiles. This trend not only improves patient outcomes but also drives efficiency and cost-effectiveness in healthcare delivery.

AI and ML have become integral to the finance industry, driving data-driven decision-making processes and improving risk management. Algorithms analyze extensive amounts of financial data to predict market trends, optimize investment portfolios, and identify potential opportunities. Fraud detection has also seen significant advancements, with ML models detecting unusual patterns in transactions and flagging potential fraudulent activities. This not only safeguards financial institutions and customers but also ensures the integrity of financial markets.

In manufacturing, AI and ML are revolutionizing operations through predictive maintenance and process optimization. Sensors and IoT devices collect real-time data from machinery, which is analyzed to predict equipment failures and maintenance needs. This approach minimizes downtime, reduces maintenance costs, and enhances overall operational efficiency. ML algorithms also optimize manufacturing processes by analyzing production data, identifying bottlenecks, and suggesting improvements, leading to increased productivity and reduced waste.

The agriculture industry is embracing AI and ML to optimize crop management and enhance productivity. Precision farming uses AI to analyze data from sensors, satellites, and drones, providing farmers with insights into soil conditions, weather patterns, and crop health. ML models predict disease outbreaks and pest infestations, allowing timely interventions. This data-driven approach improves resource allocation, minimizes environmental impact, and ensures sustainable agricultural practices.

In the retail sector, AI and ML are transforming customer experiences and inventory management. Recommendation systems analyze customer behaviors and preferences to provide personalized product recommendations, enhancing engagement and driving sales. Inventory management is optimized through demand forecasting models that analyze historical data to predict future sales patterns. This prevents stockouts and overstocking, improving supply chain efficiency and customer satisfaction.

AI and ML are shaping the energy sector by enabling the creation of smart grids and enhancing the integration of renewable energy sources. Smart grids use real-time data to balance energy supply and demand, optimizing distribution and reducing energy wastage. ML algorithms predict energy consumption patterns, allowing utilities to plan for peak loads and avoid energy shortages. Furthermore, AI-driven models optimize the integration of renewable energy sources, improving the efficiency and sustainability of energy systems.

In transportation, AI and ML are at the forefront of revolutionizing mobility through autonomous vehicles and traffic management. Self-driving cars use AI algorithms to process sensor data and navigate without human intervention. ML models predict traffic patterns, helping optimize routes and reduce congestion. This has the potential to enhance road safety, reduce emissions, and redefine urban transportation systems.

The entertainment industry leverages AI and ML to personalize content recommendations and even create new content. Streaming platforms use algorithms to analyze user preferences and viewing history, delivering tailored content suggestions. AI-driven tools also aid in content creation, generating music, art, and even writing based on learned patterns. This trend not only enhances user engagement but also accelerates content production.

The integration of AI and ML across industries is a testament to the transformative power of data-driven insights and innovation. From healthcare to entertainment, these technologies are reshaping how decisions are made, operations are optimized, and customer experiences are personalized. As industries continue to harness the potential of AI and ML, the boundaries of what's possible are expanding, and the symphony of advancements resonates in every facet of human endeavor. The legacy of AI and ML is etched in the efficiency they bring, the precision they enable, and the promise they hold for shaping a future where innovation knows no bounds.

Continuous Learning and Skill Development

Data Science and Machine Learning (or DSML) field are dynamic and rapidly evolving, driven by technological advancements, emerging methodologies, and the ever-expanding universe of data. In this section, we delve into the importance of continuous learning and skill development in DSML, exploring the reasons behind the necessity for ongoing education, the methodologies to stay current, the transformative potential it offers, and its role in shaping the future of innovation, problem-solving, and career success.

The DSML landscape is marked by constant innovation, making continuous learning a necessity. Technologies, tools, and methodologies that were cutting-edge a few years ago can quickly become outdated as new paradigms emerge. Moreover, the expanding role of DSML in various industries means that professionals must be equipped to address novel challenges and capitalize on new opportunities. Continuous learning ensures that DSML practitioners remain up-to-date with the latest techniques, algorithms, and best practices, enabling them to navigate the evolving landscape effectively.

The methodologies for continuous learning in DSML are diverse and cater to various learning styles and preferences. Online courses and MOOCs (or Massive Open Online Courses) offered by platforms like Coursera, edX, and Udacity provide structured learning paths for mastering DSML concepts. Interactive platforms like Kaggle offer hands-on experience through competitions and collaborative projects. Blogs, research papers, and academic journals are valuable resources for understanding the latest advancements. Joining DSML communities, attending conferences, and participating in webinars foster networking and exposure to diverse perspectives.

In the competitive landscape of DSML careers, lifelong learning is a crucial component of professional growth. The ability to adapt to new tools and techniques gives professionals a competitive edge in job markets. Continuous learning enhances problem-solving skills, enabling practitioners to tackle complex challenges more effectively. It also demonstrates a commitment to personal and professional growth, making individuals more attractive to employers seeking adaptable, forward-thinking team members.

The transformative potential of continuous learning in DSML is far-reaching. It empowers professionals to bridge gaps between theoretical knowledge and practical application, facilitating the translation of new techniques into real-world solutions. Continuous learners are better equipped to identify emerging trends and seize opportunities for innovation. Moreover, lifelong learners become ambassadors of change within organizations, fostering a culture of curiosity and adaptability that fuels organizational growth and competitiveness.

The evolving landscape of DSML presents ethical and societal challenges that require continuous learning to address effectively. Professionals must stay informed about the ethical implications of algorithmic bias, privacy concerns, and data security. Continuous learning equips them to develop models that are fair, transparent, and unbiased. It also enables them to contribute to discussions about the ethical use of AI and ML technologies, advocating for responsible practices that benefit society at large.

Continuous learning in DSML extends beyond the realm of technical skills. The multidisciplinary nature of DSML calls for proficiency in communication, domain knowledge, and collaboration with non-technical stakeholders. Professionals need to develop the ability to translate complex technical concepts into understandable insights for decision-makers. This interdisciplinary skill set fosters effective collaboration between DSML practitioners and domain experts, driving meaningful innovation in diverse industries.

The DSML landscape is not static; it is influenced by shifts in technology, research, and industry demands. Continuous learners are better positioned to anticipate these changes and adapt proactively. For example, as AI ethics gains prominence, professionals who engage in continuous learning can lead efforts to integrate ethical considerations into AI systems. In the face of emerging challenges such as adversarial attacks or new data privacy regulations, continuous learners can apply their updated skills to develop robust solutions.

Continuous learning and skill development are the cornerstones of success in the ever-evolving field of DSML. As the realms of data science and machine learning continue to push the boundaries of innovation, staying current is not just an option but a necessity. Continuous learners are at the forefront of transforming industries, solving complex problems, and shaping the future of technology. Their journey is marked by curiosity, adaptability, and a commitment to lifelong growth, and their legacy is etched in the transformative impact they bring to the field, the solutions they pioneer, and the uncharted territories of knowledge they explore.

CONCLUSION

Recap of Key Takeaways

Throughout this e-book, we embarked on a comprehensive journey through the multifaceted realms of Data Science and Machine Learning (DSML). From understanding the foundational concepts to exploring advanced methodologies, we uncovered the transformative power of DSML in shaping industries, driving innovation, and informing decision-making. As we conclude, let's recap the key takeaways that encapsulate the essence of our exploration.

DSML is a dynamic field that leverages data and algorithms to extract insights, make predictions, and automate decision-making processes. It encompasses a wide spectrum of techniques, from statistical analysis and machine learning algorithms to deep learning and neural networks.

Data is the bedrock of DSML. Quality data, obtained through rigorous collection, preprocessing, and cleaning, forms the basis for accurate and reliable analysis. The saying "garbage in, garbage out" underscores the importance of data quality in generating meaningful insights.

DSML follows a structured process, starting with problem definition and data collection, followed by exploratory data analysis, feature engineering, model selection, training, and evaluation. Each step contributes to the development of robust and accurate models.

Choosing the right model is critical, and the choice depends on the problem type, dataset, and desired outcome. Rigorous evaluation using appropriate metrics ensures that the chosen model performs well on unseen data.

Feature engineering involves selecting, transforming, and creating features that are relevant to the problem. Effective preprocessing techniques such as normalization, scaling, and handling missing data enhance model performance.

Machine learning algorithms range from supervised (like linear regression and decision trees) to unsupervised (like clustering) and deep learning techniques (like neural networks). The choice of algorithm depends on the nature of the problem and the available data.

DSML carries ethical responsibilities. Bias mitigation, fairness, and transparency are crucial, ensuring that algorithms do not perpetuate discrimination and that their decisions are interpretable and just.

DSML has transformative applications across industries. From healthcare's precision diagnosis to finance's risk assessment, and manufacturing's process optimization to agriculture's precision farming, the impact is far-reaching. In the ever-evolving landscape of DSML, continuous learning is paramount. Staying current with emerging trends, tools, and methodologies is crucial for professional growth and success.

The future of DSML is bright. Emerging trends like federated learning, explainable AI, and quantum machine learning hold the promise of further innovation, ethical advancement, and interdisciplinary collaboration.

In closing, this e-book has provided a panoramic view of the DSML universe. From understanding the data science process to delving into advanced concepts like neural networks and ethical considerations, we have navigated the intricacies of this transformative field. Armed with the knowledge gained, readers are equipped to embark on their own DSML journeys, shaping industries, driving innovation, and contributing to a data-powered future where possibilities are boundless and insights are infinite.

Encouragement for Further Exploration

As you journey through the captivating landscape of Data Science and Machine Learning (DSML), you've acquired a remarkable toolkit of knowledge, methodologies, and insights. Yet, this is not the end, but rather the beginning of an exciting odyssey into a world of endless possibilities and profound discoveries. Let's delve into why further exploration in DSML is not just encouraged but essential, the avenues for continued learning, and the transformative impact you can bring to the field and beyond.

DSML is akin to a river that never ceases to flow. The field is in perpetual motion, with new algorithms, tools, and techniques emerging regularly. To stay at the forefront, embracing this dynamism is imperative. Continuous learning enables you to harness the latest advancements, contributing to cutting-edge research and innovation.

DSML thrives at the intersection of various disciplines. Embracing this multidisciplinary nature opens doors to collaboration with experts from diverse fields. By integrating domain knowledge with DSML expertise, you can develop solutions that address complex challenges in healthcare, finance, sustainability, and more.

As DSML plays an increasingly integral role in society, the ethical considerations surrounding AI become paramount. By delving deeper into ethical frameworks, fairness, and transparency, you can shape AI systems that uphold moral values and contribute to a just and equitable technological landscape.

The applications of DSML are limited only by imagination. From tackling climate change through data-driven environmental solutions to revolutionizing education through personalized learning platforms, your journey in DSML empowers you to craft innovative solutions that impact the world.

The world faces intricate challenges, from global health crises to urbanization dilemmas. DSML equips you with the tools to address these complexities. By analyzing vast datasets, predicting trends, and optimizing resource allocation, you can play an active role in finding solutions to some of humanity's most pressing issues.

DSML offers fertile ground for entrepreneurship. Armed with a deep understanding of data-driven insights, you can identify market gaps and develop novel products and services that resonate with industries and consumers alike, fostering innovation and economic growth.

Your journey in DSML isn't confined to personal growth; it has the potential to inspire and educate others. Sharing your insights through blogs, workshops, and mentorship can ignite a ripple effect of learning, nurturing a community of curious minds eager to embark on their own DSML journeys.

DSML is intricately tied to the future of technology. As AI continues to revolutionize industries, your contributions have the power to shape the direction of innovation, ensuring that technological advancements are ethical, responsible, and aligned with human values.

DSML is an expedition into the unknown. The thrill of unveiling patterns, predicting outcomes, and gaining insights is akin to unraveling mysteries. Each dataset presents an opportunity for discovery, and every algorithm offers a chance to uncover insights that were once hidden.

In conclusion, the journey you've undertaken in DSML is a testament to your curiosity, dedication, and passion for unraveling the complexities of data-driven insights. But remember, this journey has no destination; it's an ongoing exploration that invites you to uncover the extraordinary, pioneer innovation, and transform industries. So, venture forth with confidence, armed with the knowledge that every step you take furthers the frontiers of DSML and contributes to a world where the power of data is harnessed for the betterment of society, science, and the human experience.

Final Thoughts on Harnessing Machine Learning for Data-Driven Decision Making

As we draw the curtains on our exploration of the intricate world of Data Science and Machine Learning (DSML), it's time to reflect on the profound impact these technologies have on data-driven decision-making. Our journey has revealed the remarkable potential of DSML to transform industries, drive innovation, and inform choices with unprecedented accuracy. In these final thoughts, we delve into the significance of harnessing machine learning for data-driven decision-making, the responsibilities it carries, and the enduring legacy it can leave in shaping a smarter, more informed world.

At the heart of DSML lies the ability to illuminate the path to precision. Through the meticulous analysis of data, machine learning models uncover patterns, trends, and insights that human cognition might overlook. These revelations guide decision-makers to make informed choices that resonate with accuracy, thereby enhancing outcomes across diverse domains.

Machine learning isn't just a tool; it's a catalyst for innovation. By mining data for hidden gems of information, organizations can unlock new avenues for products, services, and solutions. The fusion of creativity with data-driven insights generates innovation that caters to evolving market demands, enhances customer experiences, and fuels economic growth.

In an era of exponential data growth, complexity often veils the optimal course of action. Machine learning untangles this complexity, providing decision-makers with actionable insights. From healthcare diagnoses to financial risk assessment, machine learning offers clarity, enabling professionals to navigate intricate challenges with confidence.

Ethics and inclusivity are foundational to responsible decision-making. Machine learning, when coupled with ethical considerations, can help identify biases and rectify inequalities. It enables organizations to make decisions that are not only efficient but also equitable, ensuring that benefits are distributed across diverse segments of society.

The impact of machine learning isn't confined to boardrooms; it extends to shaping industries and societies. In healthcare, it advances personalized medicine. In agriculture, it optimizes crop yields. In education, it customizes learning experiences. By harnessing the power of machine learning, industries can align with societal needs and contribute to a sustainable, equitable future.

The journey in DSML underscores the importance of learning and adaptability. The ever-evolving landscape necessitates continuous learning to stay ahead. This ethos extends beyond professionals to organizations themselves, which must adapt their strategies based on real-time insights to remain competitive in an era of disruption.

Our exploration of machine learning showcases that the future is a canvas of possibilities waiting to be painted with data-driven decisions. It's a realm where algorithms sift through data, transforming it into knowledge that guides actions. It's a realm where innovation flourishes, and societies flourish in tandem.

While machine learning augments decision-making capabilities, it also carries a responsibility to use this power judiciously. As we deploy algorithms to guide choices, we must ensure transparency, accountability, and ethical considerations guide their development and application. Machine learning, when wielded responsibly, fosters trust and confidence in its outcomes.

In conclusion, our journey through the world of DSML has illuminated the transformative role machine learning plays in data-driven decision-making. From industry-specific applications to ethical considerations and the limitless potential for innovation, the legacy of harnessing machine learning resonates across sectors and influences the fabric of society. As you step forward from this journey, armed with insights and a vision for a smarter world, remember that the journey isn't over—it's merely the beginning of your impact on shaping a future where data-driven decisions pave the way for progress, innovation, and the betterment of humanity.

Thank you for buying and reading/ listening to our book. If you found this book useful/ helpful please take a few minutes and leave a review on the platform where you purchased our book. Your feedback matters greatly to us.